WHAT ARE THEY SAYING ABOUT MARY?

What Are They Saying About Mary?

Anthony J. Tambasco

PAULIST PRESS
New York/Ramsey

Library of Congress
Catalog Card Number: 84-60731

ISBN: 0-8091-2626-5

Published by Paulist Press
545 Island Road, Ramsey, N.J. 07446

Printed and bound in the
United States of America

Contents

**This book is dedicated to
my friends in the
Montfort Communities**

Preface

This book has been germinating for a long time, and I am pleased to see it finally blossom. It is written in the hope that I might be able to share the rich and fascinating symbol that Mary has become for me after my discovery of how the Bible presents her. It is written in the hope that Mary can be seen in new ways by two very distinct groups: first, by those who feel drawn to Marian piety, but are confused about its place in the present Church, and who need to renew it within a renewed and renewing Church; second, by those who feel that Marian theology and piety no longer have any significant place within the Church. I believe there is a meeting point between these two groups in the image of Mary as the perfect Christian. I believe such an image is helpful also in the ecumenical dialogue. To those who are already aware of these new approaches I hope this book will be a helpful summary of the theology.

In keeping with the nature of the series within which this book appears, I am not giving a history of Mariology, but a summary of the contemporary discussion. I refer to the history as it sheds light on the present. I have selected the Second Vatican Council as the starting point for the contemporary developments, since it is the key event which crystallized and emphasized new insights in Marian theology, as well as being also the starting point for some new insights. While I have studied and used an international bibliography, I give references only to those who have works in English, since these are the sources that will be helpful to those reading my book. In order to remain concise, I usually refer to any given work just once, although I draw on the thought of each work throughout my book.

I am grateful to Georgetown University for a summer research grant that facilitated my writing of this book. I owe special thanks to several persons who have been helpful in this work. As always, my wife Joan was encouraging and patient, especially during the long hours of the summer in which I composed much of the book. She has my love and my appreciation. My colleague Monika Hellwig was a helpful guide in my treatment of original sin and of tradition in the Church. Walter Burghardt was very gracious in taking time from an extremely busy schedule to do a detailed reading of my manuscript and to make many helpful suggestions. Last, and definitely not least, was my colleague Diane Yeager who read with great care my first draft of the book. I am grateful to her for several things: she prodded me to sharpen and clarify positions, she addressed me especially to ecumenical concerns and sensitivities, and she gave great care to refining many literary elements of the book.

Introduction
Vatican II: A New Theology

It is a well-known fact by now that the Second Vatican Council was the watershed of a movement in theology toward a new methodology leading to new emphases and even new theological insights. This renewal within the Church has affected every area of theology, but has done so at an uneven pace. Biblical studies have shown the most advanced renewal, and liturgical theology has evidenced a great deal of new emphasis and content. Moral theology, on the other hand, is still struggling to find its new bearings. Within this spectrum Marian theology has shown the pain of a new birth in ways more visible and perhaps more dramatic than other areas of theology.

The new birth has been more visible because the literature in Marian theology has undergone major shifts in both the quantity of publications and the topics discussed. The new birth has been more dramatic because Marian theology has its effects on Marian devotion, and Marian devotion has been an area of great personal involvement for Roman Catholics. Thus, the renewal in Marian theology has been acclaimed by some as long overdue and as necessary, while it has been criticized by others as a betrayal of Mary's place within God's plan of redemption.

Nevertheless, while this sometimes emotional debate has gone on, the influence of Vatican II has continued its effects. Marian theology felt its first effects negatively by a drastic reduction in Marian publication. More recently, there has been a resurgence of literature, but on new themes. Three prominent Marian theologians, E. Carroll, R. Laurentin, and G. Besutti, of the United States, France, and Italy

3

respectively, have published international bibliographies on a regular basis and indicate the changes.[1] Whereas in the past the emphasis was on the privileges of Mary, e.g., the immaculate conception, or titles such as mother of God and mediatrix, now the literature centers on the sources of Marian theology, i.e., the Scriptures, the Fathers of the Church and the teaching traditions, and on the relationship of Mary to other areas of theology such as theology of the Church, the liturgy, and the ecumenical movement. Before seeing what this literature has to say about Mary, let us take a brief overview of the major changes in method and content of Marian theology as a result of the Council.

Mariology and Use of Scripture

What happened specifically to Marian theology is parallel to what happened to theology in general as it approached the Second Vatican Council. This theology prior to the Council was faithful in handing down the traditions, but also showed a somewhat static quality. It was a theology influenced predominantly by the Council of Trent and was the last of the theology that took its direction from anti-Protestant polemic. Coming over four hundred years after the necessary and dynamic theology of Trent, the theology of the mid-twentieth century was mostly repetitive synthesis of the past in form of manuals of theology.

Taking their cue from the debate with Protestantism, these manuals sought to preserve challenged truths. Though successful in this task they also ran the risk of overemphasizing these disputed points, while undervaluing many other rich teachings of the sources of faith and while often passing over the valid and healthy points made by the Protestant Reformation itself. In the heat of polemic, opposing sides tend to exaggerate or overemphasize their side of the debate and miss the balance that can come from the joining of valid points from both sides. This polemic, as we are now to see, showed itself in a number of areas of Catholic theology, and overemphasis in these areas in turn affected the Marian theology of the time.

One of the rallying cries of the Reformation was "Scripture alone." Trent countered that by asserting the role of tradition around that Scripture. Trent did not clarify the relationship completely. A fuller elaboration would come in the theology preparatory to, and incorporated into, Vatican II. However, theology after Trent put more and more emphasis on tradition as a separate source of revelation and moved farther and farther from an adequate use of the biblical sources.

Theology in the manuals began with a systematic presentation of theses derived in large part from philosophical reasoning and went to Scripture mostly to find "proofs" of these theses. Rather than being the starting point and foundation for theological thinking, Scripture was found useful mostly to yield one or two lines of prooftext, often divorced from context. Pre-Vatican II Marian theology evidenced this same approach, with little being built on the Bible and a great deal being built on papal teaching, post-biblical traditions, and philosophical argumentation.

The writings of the prominent Marian theologians of the 1950's, which show the scholarship of the manuals of Marian theology prior to Vatican II, were collected in a three volume work edited by Juniper Carol.[2] While these works reflect the competence and talent of that time, hindsight now shows us how much of the biblical teaching was overlooked simply because other points were being stressed and because the Scriptures were not exploited to their full potential.

The tendency toward systematic organization and the proving of theses led also to fragmentation of theology into various sub-disciplines, e.g., dogmatic theology, moral theology, ascetical theology, etc. Each of the areas tended to become super-specialized, often in isolation from the other areas, and with a certain danger of self-centeredness. Marian theology felt this effect as well. It developed as a separate area, called Mariology, and gradually developed its own principles for the deduction of truths about the mother of Jesus. Moreover, since Marian theology was one of the points more sharply debated with Protestantism, it also ran the risk of being overly defensive, and of using its own proper principles in an exaggerated way.

Some evidence of the defensive use of principles of pre-Vatican II Mariology is found in the desire for that theology to achieve "new conquests." In their desire to be sure Mary was given her proper place in redemption, theologians frequently sought new titles for Mary or new prerogatives. This desire for new titles may have been part of the influence behind the definitions of the dogma of the immaculate conception in 1854 and of the assumption in 1950. While these two teachings could be seen as consistent with Christian faith, as we shall see, other developments were not so consistent. For instance, some of the distinctive Marian principles were brought to bear on new roles for Mary which encroached on other areas of theology, such as Christology. For example, the principle of analogy (Mary enjoys a role analogous to Christ), while helpful in explaining Mary's role in salvation history, came to be used less appropriately on one or another occasion to describe Mary as "mystical" head of the mystical body.

Another example of overly zealous Mariology is found in the occasionally poor use of the principle of singularity (Mary enjoys a unique role among all creatures). This principle was used to move Mary from a unique relation to Jesus in his hypostatic *union* (i.e., his personal union of divine and human natures) to some kind of objective hypostatic *order*, as if Mary bordered in some unique way on divinity. While these examples were the exception rather than the rule among Mariologists, they illustrate the need there was to draw Marian theology out of its often isolated specialization into healthy relationship to the other areas of theology.

Influence of Related Theology

Where Mariology did, as a matter of fact, relate to other areas of theology, these areas were themselves often influenced by anti-Protestant polemic. Thus, as these areas of theology came to fuller, balanced perspectives in Vatican II, they necessitated the renewal of the Mariology that built on them. For instance, the Protestant Reformation brought the cry of "grace alone" and emphasized that grace was a gift freely bestowed and totally unmerited by humanity. Theology from Trent countered by emphasizing humanity's need to respond to the gift of grace. This healthy theology gradually came to be overemphasized until it gave rise on the popular level to the impression that grace was more like a quantifiable acquisition than a personal quality created by God.

This reification of grace brought strong emphasis on meriting grace, rather than responding to it as gift. Mariology built on this notion an extensive description of Mary as "treasurer" of these merits, and such theology led to a Marian devotion that stressed petition for Mary's intercessory powers as an easy and abundant source of grace.

Marian piety before Vatican II was frequently characterized by novenas and prayers to obtain favors. Such approaches, while not unorthodox, ran the risk of superstition that one had found a sure means of merit. They also risked simply "using" Mary impersonally as a "grace dispenser" rather than treating her as a total person. As contemporary theology came to a more balanced view of grace as both gift and inner quality which can grow through response, Marian theology had to reconsider Mary's intercessory role, and Marian piety had to develop approaches to the Mother of Jesus that moved beyond simply asking her to obtain heavenly favors.

Stress on novenas and petitions flowed from another theological emphasis of the former Mariology, again influenced very much by polemics with Protestantism. The Reformers' emphasis on salvation solely by grace accepted in faith led them to the conclusion that sacraments are effective only if there is faith in those celebrating. The Council of Trent countered with a stress on the sacraments as efficacious activity of Christ independent of the faith of the recipient. No doubt both sides possessed a true but partial view of the full reality; unfortunately, these partial truths became increasingly polarized. Protestants stressed liturgy that promoted the faith experience, e.g., liturgy in the vernacular with hymns and full participation, while underplaying the theology of "real presence" and the effective action of God beyond the faith response. Catholics so stressed the efficacy of God's action in the sacraments that they saw little need for a full participatory liturgy.

Marian devotions came to partially replace the role that liturgy should have played in the faith life of Catholics. If there was little room for active participation in official liturgy, then private devotions or non-official community devotions would provide the outlet for faith expression and would foster faith development. Thus, Marian novenas and processions and other Marian devotions became the places where Catholics could sing hymns, express their prayer needs and feel themselves to be full participants in a faithful community. Vatican II brought a new emphasis to liturgy by balancing its teaching of real presence and efficacy of sacraments with the need to participate in them fully in faith. When the Eucharist became once again the central liturgical expression of faith, then there was less need for Marian devotions, and there was another reason to rethink the role of Mary in the Church.

Perhaps the most significant theological shifts that have affected Marian theology have taken place in the theology of Christ. In Christology, the interpretation of biblical sources, combined with the influence of Christian humanism speaking to a "world come of age," has led to emphasizing the humanity of Jesus, though not denying his divinity. Liberal Protestant theology moved first in this direction, while Catholic polemic put heavy stress on the divinity of Christ. In this so-called Christology "from above," where divinity is to the forefront, Mary was seen as the human face of God's relationship to us.

Mary was placed next to Christ, showing example of perfect human existence. Sometimes exaggerated Mariology would contrast Mary with Jesus, as when Mary's mercy was seen as interceding before Christ's justice, as if he could not also have mercy. Most of the time the emphasis was on Mary joined with Christ facing the community and sharing in Christ's work of redemption. Still, even while acknowledging Mary as fully and only human, Mariology paralleled a Christology "from above" with a Mariology "from above." Emphasis was on how much different and better Mary was than the rest of humanity. The desire was for new "privileges" for Mary in the form of new titles or new roles in salvation.

As Vatican II brought to the forefront a Christology "from below," it brought a new conception of the role of Mary. The devout believer no longer needed Mary as a substitute for the humanity of Christ, since that humanity of Christ was now being fully appreciated. Moreover, as Jesus was now seen as one who suffered and struggled through life just like all humanity, sin excepted, so Mary's humanity could also be developed "from below." More emphasis needed to be put on how much she is part of the Christian community, rather than apart from it. More emphasis had to be put on her faith commitment and on how she stands with the Church facing Jesus in receiving redemption. So once again, changes in related areas of theology brought new things to Marian theology after Vatican II.

The Council Document on Mary

These gradual changes in method and content that had been going on in theology and Mariology became evident at the Second

Vatican Council. As in the Marian literature and devotion that would follow the Council, the changes in Marian theology at the Council itself were more visible and dramatic than those in most other areas of theology. This fact is manifest in the fierce debate that took place between the former and the new approaches favored by different Council fathers.[3]

There was a large group of Council members who represented the methodology and the general content of Mariology as it had developed, and as we have described it, after Trent. These Council fathers wanted to continue the momentum developed by the declarations of the immaculate conception and the assumption, and sought "new conquests." Of the twenty-five hundred bishops, roughly six hundred asked explicitly that the Council say something about Mary, and four hundred requested a definition of a title or role for Mary. An entire independent document on Mary had been drafted and presented to the Council, one which represented the traditional systematic organization of doctrine somewhat distanced from Scripture, stressing Mary's privileges and building on papal teaching.

On the other hand, about one hundred bishops asked explicitly that the Council say nothing about Mary. The rest of the bishops were silent as to whether the Council should or should not speak on the subject. Vatican II eventually did speak. Indeed, other areas of theology, getting renewed treatment at the Council, would eventually bring their influence to the topic of the Mother of Jesus. By a narrow majority vote of 1,114 against 1,074, the Council fathers decided to reject the first draft and document on Mary and to produce a new text that would incorporate the significant changes in method and content that we discussed above.

The new text started from the sources of revelation, putting heavy emphasis on Scripture and relating Scripture to tradition in a more dynamic and intimate way. It moved away from more titles for Mary and sought to develop the traditional titles of Mary out of the sources of revelation, tracing Mary's role through salvation history and putting historical development into historical context. The final text of the Council kept only fourteen of the one hundred and seventeen papal quotations of the original draft and greatly increased the biblical references.

In its ecumenical spirit the Council also moved away from the previous anti-Protestant polemic sometimes associated with Mariology. It avoided any vocabulary that might prove offensive or that might be misunderstood among Protestants, e.g., titles such as "Co-Redemptrix" or "Dispensatrix of Graces." With its great stress on liturgical reform, the Council placed its encouragement of Marian devotion into the context of liturgy and gave a richer Marian piety than did the former stress on novenas and petitions alone.

Perhaps the most significant contribution of Vatican II to Marian theology was its bringing of that theology to closer relationship with Christology and with the theology of the Church. The theology of the Marian era of the 1950's prior to the Council stressed, as we have seen, a Mariology "from above," and a Mariology relating Mary by analogy to the role of Christ in redemption. It was an approach described as Christotypical in emphasis. It viewed Mary as joined with Christ facing the Church in the work of redemption and tended to keep Mary distinct from the Church and from Christians.

Vatican II often sought compromises between conflicting schools of thought, so it did not reject this Christotypical approach. Thus, the chapter on Mary in the text *Lumen Gentium* devotes the first section (numbers 55–59) to the Christotypical approach. This method is toned down, however, since the text deliberately does not define the nature of Mary's cooperation with Jesus in redemption, and avoids new titles and privileges that would tend to further distinguish Mary from the rest of creation. In the rest of the document the Council stresses another approach to Mary, a Mariology "from below," and connects her more intimately with Christians and the Church. This approach is called ecclesiotypical and tends to stress Mary as joined to the Church facing Christ and being redeemed by Christ who is the all-sufficient mediator of salvation.

Vatican II did not claim to answer all the questions of a new Marian theology, nor did it attempt to fully resolve the conflict between the two approaches to Mary. It rather indicated the risks of a speculative, defensive, or over-specialized Mariology, and the benefits of a balanced approach that would keep Mary totally subordinate to Christ and member of the Church even as one searched for her particular role in salvation history. The strongest confirmation of this message came from the decision concerning the placement of the Council's text on Mary.

It was a hotly debated issue, for it was linked to the differences between the two approaches to Mariology. When the first draft document on Mary was rejected by a narrow margin, so was the plan to issue a separate document on Mary. The Council fathers decided to put the text as chapter eight in the document on the Church, *Lumen Gentium.* Ultimately, while the first decisions about the document were based on narrow voting margins, the final text of chapter eight was accepted by a vote of 2080 to 10. It was a stirring affirmation of a Marian theology with renewed method and content. It said by its very location that theology of Mary needs to be inserted into the context of other theology and that Mary needs to be seen not simply next to Jesus in some qualified way in the work of redemption, but also within the Church as fully redeemed herself.

Marian literature and Marian devotion since Vatican II have for the most part followed the lead of the Council. As Marian theology begins to grow again after a period of decline, it is marked by new methods and much new content. We turn now to more detailed description of what they are saying about Mary.

1
Mary in Scripture: History

Perhaps the richest discovery of a renewed Mariology has been within the area of Scripture, which has offered new themes and provided the foundation for new theological elaborations and new kinds of devotion. There is still the consideration of Christotypical themes, e.g., the study of Mary's motherhood and its relation to Christ's role in redemption. The new insights, however, have come predominantly in the ecclesiotypical themes which show Mary as the perfect disciple receiving redemption from her Son and responding to his gifts. The Bible texts with important Marian content are found chiefly in the infancy narrative of Luke 1—2 and in the stories of Cana and Calvary in John 2 and 19. The other passages which contain some significant Marian teaching are Matthew 1:18–25 (Mary's conception of Jesus), Mark 3:31–35 and 6:1–6, and the parallels to these two texts (Mary and the family of Jesus), Acts 1:14 (Mary at Pentecost), and Revelation 12 (the woman and the dragon).

Major works which survey most of the New Testament literature pertaining to Mary and which reflect these new themes include books by John McHugh,[1] Lucien Deiss[2] and Max Thurian,[3] the latter being of particular interest because the author is a Protestant. Raymond Brown has done an extensive study of the infancy narratives,[4] as well as of John's Gospel,[5] and so has covered most of the biblical material dealing with Mary. Finally, a study by a task force of New Testament scholars in the Lutheran-Catholic dialogues has gathered up much of the biblical discussion and presented an ecumenical survey of the themes.[6]

The focal point of these biblical studies has been, as we indicated, ecclesiotypical themes regarding Mary. This means, for the most part, a Mariology "from below," stressing Mary's identity with humanity, her need for redemption, and especially her faith which opened her to receive that redemption. Such an approach harmonizes with the approach to Christ "from below," and both approaches result from current insight into the nature of biblical literature. Contemporary biblical scholars have noted that the Gospels as we have them are written in the hindsight of the resurrection of Jesus and so retroject into the story of the public life of Jesus all the insights gained from that climax of the public life. It seems reasonable to assume, therefore, that many of the definitive claims of Jesus, e.g., to divinity, are not so much biographical reports from the earthly Jesus as theological statements of the risen Jesus retrojected into the public life.

This biblical interpretation has led to a Christology "from below," for it enables study of this human Jesus of the public life, who is distinct from what he will become as the risen Christ. Such a Christology certainly appreciates the ultimate teachings of divinity and other aspects of the risen Jesus. Nevertheless it also finds it fruitful to reflect on the very human way in which Jesus arrived at the final teachings. Historical criticism is applied to the Gospels to distinguish passages that seem most likely to be retrojection from resurrection hindsight. Effort is made to detect those elements that would probably have come from the actual history of Jesus. These elements are joined to scholarly assumptions about the way a human being would experience life. The end result gives us a portrait of Jesus. If such a view of Jesus is accurate, he becomes like us in all things except sin. It seems likely that he did not consciously know of his divinity until death and resurrection, and his life is one with which we can identify: a pilgrimage of trust and obedience until victory and insight in the resurrection.[7]

The Quest for the Historical Mary

Ecclesiotypical Mariology takes its cue from this particular Christology and begins also from insights into the nature of biblical literature. There is the recognition that almost all of the texts that speak of Mary are located in precisely those parts of the Gospels that are least concerned with being historically accurate, namely, the infancy narrative of Luke and the entire Gospel of John. As we have said, all of the Gospels are concerned not so much with history as with the interpretation of history, the meaning of the events for salvation. When one approaches the infancy stories of Luke and the entire Gospel of John, one finds even less concern with exact history and more concern with interpretation. Moreover, the hindsight of the full revelation that comes from the resurrection seems retrojected into these stories even more than in the rest of the Gospels.

Luke's infancy narrative (Lk 1—2) has visions and apparitions quite out of character in the stories of the public life. The visions are joined to other stories which are woven mostly out of Old Testament images and events. They all proclaim at the beginning of the Gospel what will actually be the clear results at the end in the resurrection event. They make the clearest statements in the Gospels about the person and mission of Jesus, statements that make sense when one has discovered the risen Christ. Likewise, John's Gospel proves to be almost totally different from the Synoptics in chronology, content and its portrayal of Jesus' person. It shows itself to be a long meditation on the meaning of Jesus' life and person. Events are redescribed and reinterpreted to show Jesus reflecting the life of God himself. This is a long meditation in the hindsight of the resurrection.

If this is the nature of the biblical texts that speak of Mary, then it seems highly probable that what is said of her is said in the hindsight of the resurrection. We find in Luke and in John a theological description of Mary who stands at the fullness of her human perfection, sharing fully in the life of the risen Lord. We can be less sure of how much of this description records actual events in the history of Mary prior to the resurrection and the theology of the early Church. We have in the quest for the historical Mary a parallel but exacerbated version of the problem of searching for the historical Jesus. Whereas in the quest for the history of Jesus we have abundant material to work with, in the quest for the historical Mary we have only those texts that are highly theological in nature and further removed from historical concerns.

In the light of this evidence certain scholars such as the task force of the Lutheran-Catholic dialogues have concluded that each of the Marian texts has to be judged on its own merits, and that the nature of these texts puts the burden of proof on those who would assert historicity. Raymond Brown has said explicitly that "the New Testament does not give us much knowledge of Mary as an historical character."[8] Brown continues to say, however, that this is not a negative point, since what is more important is the symbol of Mary as woman of faith and type of Christian discipleship. In the same vein the Lutheran-Catholic task force has observed that it is less important whether Mary was historically the first disciple than that Luke makes her the first. From the time of the resurrection and in the development of the full faith perspectives of the early Church, Mary stood as pre-eminent among the disciples. We have little knowledge of actual events in her life, but we do have insight into her attitudes of faith. That is the way in which she is described in the Bible, and that is the way in which she remains important for the Church.

Granted that this is the heart of the biblical data, the question still arises of whether these attitudes of Mary began only after the resurrection. The late Dominic Unger took strong exception to Brown's viewpoint, and insisted that the biblical accounts record historical events.[9] His arguments were based mostly on the authority of Pope Paul VI, who he claimed understood the texts as historical facts. The argument does not face directly the nature of the biblical texts, and does not distinguish between the Pope's *use* of biblical texts to exhort to faith and his authoritative *judgment* on the historicity of the texts themselves. It does not seem from the statements cited by Unger that the Pope intended to answer the question of historicity in either direction. Nevertheless, Unger made a sound observation when he reminded us that history and symbol are not contradictories and that an historical event itself can be a symbol.

James Reese sums up an approach that finds in the biblical texts a portrait of Mary faithful to what she was like in history even before the resurrection, but which does not imitate Unger's attempts to find each story portraying historical fact.[10] According to Reese, a story can convey the *meaning* of historical events without giving any of the actual *facts* of what happened. John McHugh agrees with this observation, distinguishing between reporting events that happened and reporting events exactly as they happened. This approach has the advantage of recognizing the symbolic nature of the stories involving Mary, while also acknowledging that the symbols describe Mary as she lived during the infancy, public life, and death of Jesus. One can and should distinguish those elements of Mary's faith that would clearly have developed after the resurrection of Jesus, but it is not necessary to say that all of Mary's faith begins only after that resurrection.

Even exegetes who would be more cautious about affirming anything of the historical Mary hesitate to say that the symbols come totally out of theological imagination with no foundation in the real person of Mary. Moreover, there is some continuity between the personalities of the public life of Jesus and the believers of the early Church, just as there is some continuity between the historical Jesus and the risen Lord. The Lutheran-Catholic task force notes that while there is good evidence that Mary remained with her family and did not actively follow Jesus as a disciple during his public life, there is also no verse in the New Testament which ever says that Mary did not believe. It is not a great step to further conclude that the biblical text presents the attitudes of a Mary who lived faith all during her history, although the text does not record many events of that history. Moreover, in the biblical concern this historical image is secondary, for the text concentrates on the full flowering of Mary's faith in the hindsight of the resurrection of her Son.

Mary's Knowledge of Jesus' Divinity

One of the areas of historical research on Mary that has undergone noticeable change concerns the question of whether Mary knew of the divinity of her Son.[11] In the past varied answers were given, depending on which texts the exegetes focused on.[12] Those who took a text such as the annunciation scene stressed that the angel revealed titles that were equivalent to divine identification of Jesus (Lk 1:35). Those who took a text such as the finding of the child in the temple stressed that the parents are described as not yet understanding what their child Jesus was about (Lk 2:41–52). Current scholarship has come to recognize that all these texts are symbolic stories and that one cannot take any of the conversation in the stories as biographical detail. Moreover, assumptions about how faith operated in a human Mary would lead one to presume that her insights had to grow over history. That makes it likely that insights into the divinity of Christ as they appear now in the infancy narratives are retrojections into the story of Mary only in the hindsight of the resurrection of Jesus.

The principle of analogy may also give insight here. If it makes sense to develop a Christology "from below" and to conclude that even Jesus did not have full insight into his divinity until his resurrection, then it makes sense to develop a Mariology "from below" which would have to assume that Mary could not know more than Jesus during the public life. This debate in Mariology depends very strongly on the debate in Christology, and we have seen that a Christology which takes seriously the humanity of Jesus is more and more the prevalent emphasis. Thus, more and more exegetes are becoming comfortable with the view that Mary did not learn of the divinity of her Son until after his resurrection. This does not mean that we can do a biography or psychology of Mary to pinpoint what she knew at what stage of her earthly life. We can only speak of generalities and probabilities. Mary's faith revealed to her all that she needed to know at each stage of her journey in God's plan, but it was not necessary that she know the final outcome until it arrived.

Some would wonder how this lack of knowledge could be reconciled with the virginal conception of Jesus by Mary. Would not the virgin birth indicate to Mary the divinity of her Son? An adequate answer would first have to address the question of whether the virginity of Mary is historical fact or theological symbol. We will do this presently. Suffice it to say for now that even if one grants the historical facticity of the virginal conception and birth, it would not necessitate Mary's full knowledge of her Son's divinity. Could she not find herself miraculously with child and simply make a firm act of faith and trust that this was of God? This act of trust would have been her first step in a long journey. The final meaning of that virgin birth and the object of her trust would have come clear only in the resurrection of her Son and the fruition of faith of the early Church. It would seem once again that there is good argument that Mary did not know of the divinity of Jesus from the very beginning.

The Virginity of Mary

Another area of intense debate related to the historical Mary is over the question of her virginity. Are the virginal conception and birth of Jesus and the perpetual virginity of Mary part of the historical data of Scripture or a symbolic statement pointing to some theological truth of another order? Such a question was not even asked until modern biblical scholarship revealed the nature of the Gospel literature and allowed distinctions between historical facts and interpretative symbols. Protestant exegetes moved first to question Mary's virginity as historical fact, though there is debate even among them.[13] Within Roman Catholicism the controversy developed only after Vatican II, and, of course, acquired a particular Catholic flavoring. Raymond Brown brought the discussion to the English-speaking world and offered important summaries of the debate.[14]

Many Catholic exegetes have confessed that the perpetual virginity of Mary, while never defined in a solemn, extraordinary, infallible way, is nevertheless an infallible teaching of the ordinary magisterium of the Church. Still, they would contend, there is room for questioning, since ordinary teaching of the Church is more difficult to pinpoint than the solemn, extraordinary declarations. The questioning can move in two directions. One can ask whether theologians have been accurate in ascribing this teaching to the category of infallible truth, since Mary's virginity could in fact simply have been *assumed* to be historical without anyone ever determining the issue definitively. The other line of questioning would ask whether the credal formulae, like "born of the Virgin Mary," intended to confess truths about Jesus' human reality without intending to define the historicity of the virginal conception as part of the teaching. In other words, could the ordinary teaching in its creeds be doing exactly what Scripture could be doing in its statements on the virginal conception, i.e., using it as symbol to convey other truths of revelation? Again, the Church could have *presumed* the historicity of the virginity, but now that presumption needs to be asked about directly.

Because of these possibilities of questioning, Catholic biblical scholars have begun to re-examine the biblical data in this particular search for the historical Mary. The biblical investigation is actually being carried out on two points, because of the way the doctrine has generally been taught. Church formulation has expressed Mary's virginity as *before birth* (virginal conception), *at birth* (miraculous delivery), and *after birth* (perpetual virginity). The virginity of Mary at birth is a doctrinal debate beyond the Bible, so it does not enter into exegetical deliberations. (We will consider it briefly at the end of this section.) The other two aspects have referents in the Bible and are points of debate among scholars today.

Virginity before Birth

The bulk of recent literature has concentrated on Mary's virginal conception of Jesus (virginity before birth). A few Catholic authors, including for example Louis Evely,[15] join the Protestants who deny this virginity as an historical fact and assert that it is a symbol pointing to other theological truths. A large number of Catholic scholars, including McHugh in his major work, and John Craghan and Geoffrey Graystone who have written major works on this particular topic,[16] opt for the historicity of the virginal conception of Jesus. Nevertheless, some very formidable scholars have concluded that the Scriptures leave the historicity an open question that probably will not be decided on the biblical evidence alone. This group includes Raymond Brown (though he thinks the evidence for historicity gives rise to fewer problems of interpretation and seems more likely) and Joseph Fitzmyer,[17] who are joined by the rest of the Lutheran-Catholic task force of which they are members.

The first reason for doubting the historicity of Mary's virginal conception of Jesus is, as we have mentioned, the heavily symbolic nature of the infancy narratives. The virginal conception of Jesus points to such an exalted view of who he is that it bears the marks of post-resurrection hindsight and theology. The evidence is compounded by the fact that the virginal conception is not mentioned anywhere else in the New Testament. Manuel Miguens has claimed to find evidence in Mark, Paul and John for the virginal conception, but scholars have generally faulted him with having a doctrinal bias that causes him to read into the text what is not there.[18]

One can affirm that there is at least a doubt that the virginity of Mary was held from the beginning as a universal teaching in all the New Testament churches. This conclusion also raises doubts that the virginal conception was a fact handed down by Jesus' family to become part of the foundational faith, and to be universally accepted by the early Christians. Thus, there is also a possibility that the communities who did speak of the virginity of Mary in the infancy narratives introduced it as a theological symbol to point to the theology of Christ that they were developing.

Current scholars who maintain the historicity of the virginal conception do so with some strong arguments. It is not likely that the virginity is a symbol, for we would most likely find parallel symbols in comparable stories about the origins of famous religious personalities. Now the virginity seems a unique kind of detail which finds no exact parallel, at least no parallel in the literature that would have been accessible to the early Christians, whether in Jewish or Hellenistic circles. It seems more likely that such a unique feature would then have come because it was part of the historical facts.

There seems to be confirming evidence within the Scriptures themselves. The only texts that give clear affirmation of the virginal conception of Jesus are in Matthew's infancy narrative (1:18–25) and Luke's infancy narrative (1:26–38). The fact can be granted that these stories, like the rest of the infancy stories, are heavily symbolic. It is curious, however, that while the stories of Matthew and Luke differ in almost all their content, they agree on the virginal conception. This is probably because of history, especially when it would have been easier for both authors *not* to speak of this fact, were it only a symbol. For example, why should Matthew, so concerned with paternal genealogy, suddenly present Jesus conceived without a father? Why would Luke, who has been comparing the annunciations regarding John and Jesus, leave one massive difference instead of comparing the fathers? We probably have the force of history behind these details of the stories, even if much else is symbol.

Unfortunately, the debate does not end here. Those who raise doubts sometimes grant the fact that Matthew and Luke took the virginity of Mary to be historical. However, they say that these two evangelists intended primarily to make Christological statements, that they *presumed* the virginity of Mary to be true as they took it over from their theological sources in the post-resurrection community, but that the rest of the New Testament casts doubts on whether their presumption can be verified. Thus, the debate on the biblical level concerning the virginity *before birth* remains unresolved at this time, and biblical scholars admit that their evidence may never be sufficient to conclude the arguments.

One aspect of this search for history, however, seems to be reaching fuller consensus. Despite continued attempts by exegetes such as Graystone to promote the affirmative opinion, more and more biblicists agree that Mary did not make a vow of virginity before the annunciation. Much has revolved around the interpretation of Luke 1:34, Mary's question, "How shall this be, since I have no husband?" In the past there was much debate over whether the question indicated that Mary had previously taken a vow, or whether the question expressed simple surprise or even protest.

Present insight has concluded that the question cannot be taken as biographical in any case. It is a literary device by Luke to prepare the way for the Christological answer which is what he intends to teach in the story. The format is borrowed from annunciation stories frequent in the Old Testament. Moreover, it seems that the desire to find a vow in the story comes more from a Mariology "from above" which tends to stress Mary's difference from humanity at large. An ecclesiotypical Mariology and one "from below" tends to see Mary as part of her culture and as growing in faith gradually. She cannot be expected to have made a decision so contrary to that of pious Jewish girls of her time.

Virginity after Birth

While it would seem unlikely that Mary made a vow before the annunciation, even a Mariology "from below" would acknowledge the possibility of her making a vow after the conception and the birth of Jesus. The debate at present is whether this perpetual virginity of Mary is historical fact or theological symbol. Many more Protestants, including those who maintained the historicity of the virginal conception, part company with Roman Catholics on this issue, and hold that Mary subsequently lived a normal marriage with Joseph and may even have had other children. Much revolves around the interpretation of passages such as Mark 6:3 and its parallels, which speak of the "brothers and sisters" of Jesus and even name some.

Actually, there are no really new and startling arguments that have not generally been advocated from the time of St. Jerome and his debate with Helvidius, but there is the movement of a few Roman Catholics away from Jerome's interpretation and the classical Catholic view.[19] The arguments are still that the word "brothers" means either blood-brothers, or step-brothers (children of Joseph by a previous marriage), or cousins. John McHugh lines up all the arguments in a lengthy section of his major work on Mary and concludes with a novel twist that the "brothers" were first cousins on Joseph's side rather than the usual theory of cousins on Mary's side. (McHugh also finds evidence of Mary's perpetual virginity in the annunciation scene. He believes that the question of Mary in Luke 1:34, which we discussed above, is indeed Luke's literary device. It does not indicate a vow of Mary *antecedent* to conception. However, Luke words the question in precisely this way because he knows that *afterward* Mary will remain a virgin. Thus, the annunciation scene anticipates the perpetual virginity of Mary. While the argument of McHugh is ingenious, he seems not to have attracted many followers.)

The arguments about Mary's virginity after birth, like those about virginity before birth, do not remove all doubt. It can be said with assurance that the New Testament does not raise directly the question of Mary's perpetual virginity after the birth of Jesus. The problem of determining the exact relationship of the "brothers and sisters" of Jesus arose only in later history when the Church began preaching the perpetual virginity of Mary. Even if one establishes the relatives as cousins, it constitutes only partial evidence that Mary remained a virgin. How one approaches the texts depends in large part on what one thinks of later Church teaching. Even if one maintains the perpetual virginity of Mary, it is legitimate to ask the question whether this teaching of the ordinary magisterium posits historical fact or theological symbol which has simply been presumed to be historical.

Virginity at Birth

One final area of historical research has involved Mary's virginity at the birth of Christ, and asks whether this birth entailed a miraculous delivery, free from pain and without opening the womb. Arguments here revolve around what constitutes virginity. The doctrine seems to intend that the birth of Jesus did not impair Mary's virginity, but the doctrine also operates under the impression that virginity requires an unopened womb and not just voluntary abstinence from sexual relations. It further insists so heavily on preserving Mary's virginity that it seems to infringe on her genuine motherhood. Moreover, there is no warrant in Scripture for a miraculous delivery, while there is to believe that Mary shared our human condition by normal childbirth.

Many scholars today who accept the formula of Mary's virginity before, at and after birth understand it to mean Mary's virginity throughout life. They further conclude that singling out the stage "at birth" hearkens to an era which had a particular (and inadequate) view of virginity and thus falsely presumed there was need to single out this stage. It seems that the full intent of the doctrine, and even the historicity of Mary's virginity, can be maintained without taking this part of the formula literally.[20]

We conclude this treatment of the historicity of Mary's virginity with some summary remarks. Because of the confusion of biblical evidence, it seems legitimate to raise the question of historicity on this topic. The biblical evidence in the final analysis seems not conclusive. Most Roman Catholic scholars, even if they leave the issue now as an open question, would acknowledge that the Church could clarify the issue with a solemn declaration. In that case, however, one must recognize that the doctrine is a step beyond the biblical data and that further authority must be recognized. In keeping these distinctions clear, one avoids the risk of reading teaching into the Bible and of having the Bible say more than it intends to say. It also seems reasonable to suppose that even if one accepts the virginity of Mary as historical, one should interpret the biblical reasons for that virginity as truths that come clear only after the resurrection and that are retrojected into the infancy narratives.

The biblical debates that have evolved recently over this issue of virginity have had the merit at least of separating the doctrine from its false identity with other doctrines and have exposed arguments for Mary's virginity from the wrong reasons. Some, for instance, have said that Mary's virginity is necessary to maintain her sinlessness or to maintain the sinlessness of Jesus. In the same vein, some have fought for Mary's virginity because of a poor theology which saw celibacy as the way of perfection and marriage as somehow inferior. This comes from a poor view of sexuality which somehow associates sexual relations with sin or with original sin. Moreover, if sex can be seen in a good light, then Jesus could have been born from normal sexual intercourse and still been free from all sin. Others have claimed that the divinity of Jesus demands virginal conception, a claim which again falsely links the two doctrines, since Jesus could have been born of human relations and still been divine.

Once these false arguments are removed, much of the emotion surrounding the historicity of Mary's virginity is defused. Then what becomes central are the theological reasons for her virginity in the first place. Strangely enough, those reasons are primarily Christological rather than Mariological, i.e., they say something about Jesus even more than about Mary. The virginity of Mary is a sign that God has intervened in our history with a new creation and that redemption is his work, not ours. Virginity points in a visible way to the uniqueness of Jesus who has entered our history. It is not necessary for his divinity, but it is a forceful sign of that divinity. Finally, virginity may be a sign of Mary's consecration to God, though that does not seem the stress of the biblical texts.

Ultimately, this meaning of Mary's virginity is the same meaning understood by those who do not accept that virginity as historical. No one denies that there is meaning in the doctrine of Mary's virginity. Some affirm that meaning as coming simply from a symbol in the text. Those who affirm an historical fact simply posit a stronger symbol. In the long run that may be the crucial question of Mary's virginity. All can come to agree on what it symbolizes. Our continuing questions concern the strength of the symbol. Is Mary's virginity purely symbol, or is it an actual historical fact that bears the same symbolism?

2
Mary in Scripture: Symbol

Most of what we discussed in the preceding chapter is actually of secondary importance to the biblical authors, as important as it is to us. Even for contemporary theology the quest for the historical Mary is simply a starting point. What is of central concern both for the Bible and for the present is the theological description of Mary's place in the mystery of redemption. The biblical concern was to express the attitude of the first Christians toward Mary and to reflect her attitudes toward Christ and his unfolding mystery. We have mentioned previously that contemporary understanding of the biblical material results in a portrait of Mary that reflects an ecclesiotypical Mariology. We need now to get an overview of the principal themes as these are expounded by contemporary scholars, especially those scholars mentioned at the beginning of the last chapter.

The underlying thought that unifies the biblical themes is the symbol of Mary as the perfect Christian. For the reasons articulated in the last chapter, we will assume that the faith attitudes of Mary were actually lived all during her history. Nevertheless, we must also recall that the texts convey her attitudes, but not necessarily the actual events, and we will assume, along with most scholars, that the stories are primarily symbolic stories getting to those attitudes. The texts will convey the attitudes of the historical Mary before the resurrection of Jesus, when they give hints of an incipient faith or a developing faith, e.g., where Mary has still to realize fully who her Son is. We will also recognize, however, that most of the elements of the biblical portrait express attitudes of Mary in the hindsight of resurrection. The Jesus described in most stories, even those seemingly before his death, is the Christ known fully because of his resurrection. Thus, the faithful Mary described in these stories has as the object of her faith the risen Jesus. We have as it were the "finished product" of Mary showing the attitudes of every Christian who unites to Christ as risen Lord.

Woman of Faith in Luke

The basic attitudes of Mary described in the New Testament are indicated especially in Luke's Gospel. As we consider these texts, we will observe that the portrait of Mary was one that developed gradually, since Luke's description of Mary advances considerably beyond Mark's, and since in Luke there is development in the description of Mary from the simple accounts of the public life to the more elaborate stories of the infancy narrative. We will begin with Luke's simple stories of Mary in the public life of Jesus, then we will compare them with Mark's, and finally we will show the relationship of these stories to the stories of Luke's infancy narrative.

The pattern found in most of the biblical texts for describing Mary's attitudes is established in a study of Luke 8:19–21. The scene recounts how Jesus, when told that his "mother and brothers" are outside, says, "My mother and my brothers are those who hear the word of God and do it." With this short passage Luke says that what is important for Mary is not her physical relationship to Jesus, but her relationship of faith. The scene takes on more meaning and may show the developing attitudes of the early Church toward Mary, when it is compared with the scene in Mark 3:31–35.

In Mark's telling of the story Jesus seems to be contrasting his mother with those who have faith in him. For one thing, Mark explicitly mentions that Jesus looked on those around him (in contrast to his family outside), and said these are his true mother and brothers because of faith. For another thing, Mark has prepared for this contrast by telling a prior story (3:20–21) in which Jesus' family (including Mary?) thought he was crazy. Authors debate whether Mark shows hostility between Jesus and his mother or simply neutrality. In either case we seem to have a passage composed before a high estimate of Mary established itself.

Luke's church seems to reflect this development. Writing about fifteen years after Mark, Luke removes the contrast in his story. He makes no mention of Jesus looking on the insiders in contrast to his mother outside, and he omits the disparaging story that Mark told previously. Thus, the important relationship to Jesus is not blood relation, but faith. However, Mary is the primary example of this, for she hears the word of God and keeps it. In fact, to make sure that readers appreciate his point Luke writes another story that is almost a doublet of this one and which appears only in Luke's Gospel. In Luke 11:27–28, when a woman praises Mary for the womb that bore Jesus, he replies that the important praise is for those who hear the word of God and keep it. If this story parallels the other, then Luke does not intend to exclude Mary, but rather to offer her as first example of the Christian who keeps God's word.

We have described these stories as the pattern for Marian biblical texts, because the central point of these stories is the most frequent point of most of the rest of biblical literature about Mary. Raymond Brown gives an overview of the biblical texts from this perspective.[1] Brown maintains that the stories of Mary in the infancy narratives are not biographical. They are built up by Luke from the two scenes which we have been considering in Luke's Gospel. These infancy stories are designed to anticipate at the beginning of the Gospel the same image of Mary that is in the public life. The third Gospel illustrates from the beginning that Mary hears the word of God and keeps it (8:19–21), for Luke's story of the annunciation stresses Mary's final consent, "Let it be to me according to your word" (1:38). Likewise, in 1:39–45, Elizabeth dramatizes in the story of the visitation all the dialogue between Jesus and the woman in 11:27–28. Elizabeth says, "Blessed is the fruit of your womb," but concludes by saying also, "Blessed is she who believed . . . what was spoken to her from the Lord."

Woman of Faith in John

The two principal texts in which John speaks of Mary seem to emphasize the same point that we have been discussing. According to many scholars, the story of the wedding feast at Cana (Jn 2:1–11) seems to be John's adaptation and reinterpretation of a popular story about Jesus that circulated in the early Church. Originally the story was probably similar to many of those that found their way into the apocryphal or false gospels. These did not have good theological content and were designed simply to satisfy curiosity about the boyhood and family life of Jesus. Often the stories were of miracles, not to make sound theological points, but to entertain and to make an impression. Thus, the original story most likely told of how Jesus, his friends and mother went to a family wedding. The wine ran out, the mother of Jesus told the servants to follow Jesus' directions, and he impressed all with an abundance of wine.

John took this idle story, added dialogue to it, and made a strong theological statement. As the story unfolds and the wine runs out, Mary in effect asks Jesus to perform a miracle for his mother and family. One would think that the importance of Mary is based on her physical motherhood. But Jesus responds to that presupposition. His relation to Mary and to all his family is no longer the blood relationship: "Woman, what have you to do with me?" (2:4). Miracles are to be part of his public revelation and to point ultimately to his death and resurrection: "My hour has not yet come." Then Mary understands that she must stress a relationship of faith to her Son. When she tells the servants to do what Jesus says, she implicitly asks Jesus to begin his public ministry and to anticipate the hour. She wants him to work a miracle, but now no longer to do his mother a favor, but to begin his revelation with "the first of his signs" (2:11). And Mary is the first to believe, even before Jesus works the sign.

To diverge from John for a moment here, and to return to Luke, scholars observe that Luke's story of the finding of Jesus in the temple (2:41–52) exhibits traits similar to John's Cana scene. Luke may have taken a curiosity story about childhood, originally designed to impress people (the amazing knowledge of the child), and transformed it into a theological statement. The dialogue is much like that in John's story. Mary (and Joseph) are concerned for Jesus as the natural, blood relatives. Jesus changes the relationship by his question, "Did you not know I must be in my Father's house?" From now on the relationship must be one of faith in Jesus as the revelation of God.

To return to John, we observe that what he has taught about Mary at the beginning of his Gospel, he affirms again at the end in the other scene where Mary figures prominently, at the foot of Calvary (19:25–27). The use again of "woman" to address Mary, plus

the fact that actual names are not used for the mother or the beloved
disciple, indicates that John is concerned primarily with expressing
new ties between Jesus and Mary and symbolic roles for both Mary
and the disciple. Throughout John's Gospel the beloved disciple represents the community of the Fourth Gospel, which sees itself as the
object of Jesus' special love. Now, as Jesus moves from death to resurrection, he leaves in the symbol of the beloved disciple a community
of faith. John also wants to say that Mary relates to Jesus primarily
in that same faith relationship, so Mary is given as mother to the community symbolized by the beloved disciple. In his own way John says
what Luke did, that the mother and brothers of Jesus are not so much
his natural family as those who believe. This does not exclude the natural mother of Jesus, but sees her as prime exemplar of the believer
in the community born from the cross.

From all that we have just seen, we can conclude that the principal passages which speak of Mary emphasize that she holds primary
place among Christians above all because of her faith. We may conjecture that she had an incipient faith at the conception of her Son,
that it was challenged and grew during his public life, and that it
matured at his death. We recognize that the annunciation and visitation scenes may be symbolic stories, as may be Cana and the
description of Mary at Calvary. We may surmise that Mary had some
inner experience of faith that offers the historical roots of the annunciation story. We may presume that she did appear on Calvary with
a further insight of faith. These things we cannot know for certain.
What is sure is that Mary eventually came to be symbol of the believ-
ing post-resurrection community. Luke's infancy stories and John's
stories tell of the risen Jesus, and of Mary who relates to him as all
Christians must. She is woman of faith.

Old Testament Symbols

The New Testament, especially Luke's infancy narrative, also
describes Mary's faith and her relationship to Christ by portraying
Mary in Old Testament images. Luke enjoys taking the faith-filled
personalities of the Old Testament and the themes that reflect God's
work in Israel, and he weaves them into stories that show Mary as
personification and culmination of these images. In their books men-

tioned in the previous chapter, Deiss and Thurian focus on this message of Luke, but the other authors whom we have mentioned also give abundant treatment to this topic. McHugh begins his work with a specific analysis of this aspect of Luke's method.

The entire infancy narrative of Luke is described as midrash, i.e., a use of Old Testament texts by interpreters who came after the writing of these texts, to show their application to some situation in the present, and thus to show some relevant point not perhaps obvious to the present reader of the Old Testament. This use of Scripture is not concerned, as is modern biblical interpretation, with getting the intention of the authors of the Old Testament. The concern is, rather, to explain the text with relevancy for the present circumstances. It is a homiletic interpretation. Illustrations are found in Galatians 4:21–31 and 1 Corinthians 10:1–13. McHugh acknowledges that the definition of midrash does not fit exactly with Luke's purpose, for Luke wants to explain the present (of Jesus) in the light of the past (Old Testament), not to explain the meaning of the past for the present. Nevertheless, there seems a midrashic quality to the infancy texts in their description of Jesus and Mary in Old Testament images.

One of the midrashes shows Mary as reliving in an eminent way the roles of Abraham and Sarah. In the Magnificat which she prays (Lk 1:46–55), Mary proclaims that God has remembered his mercy to Abraham. Abraham had faith and, because of that, became the father of a nation. Mary's faith leads to the one who will be the final blessing for all nations. There needs to be God's intervention. Abraham and Sarah both asked, "Shall Sarah who is ninety bear a child?" (Gen 17:17 and 18:12); Mary asks, "How shall this be done?" (Lk 1:34). Yet Mary surpasses Sarah in faith, for Sarah needed to be challenged: "Is anything too hard for the Lord?" (Gen 18:14), while Mary was confirmed in her conviction: "Nothing will be impossible with God" (Lk 1:37). Whereas Sarah laughed, Mary showed joyful acceptance and total obedience. She is again the woman of faith.

Further Old Testament images surrounding Mary's conception show the object of her faith to be extraordinary, indeed, and the prototype of the faith of every Christian. The angel's annunciation in Luke 1:32–33, is a paraphrase of 2 Samuel 7:8–16, where David is promised a great name, a throne and kingdom forever, and a dynasty that will be blessed by God as a son. Now Jesus is seen as that Son of the Most High, who is great, and who has a throne and kingdom forever. Mary's faith is in Jesus as Messiah, the culmination of Davidic expectations. Yet Mary's faith, like that of all Christians, is in a Jesus who is more than what the Old Testament expected. Her offspring is described as virginally conceived by the power of the Spirit, a sign of the uniqueness of this child, and the object of her faith is seen as ultimately the Son of God himself (Lk 1:35).

There are two other Old Testament images attributed to Mary, namely those of the daughter of Zion and the ark of the covenant. These images are seen by McHugh, Deiss, Thurian and a host of biblical scholars as prominent in Luke's infancy narrative, but are doubted by Brown, the rest of the Lutheran-Catholic task force, and a number of other scholars. The daughter of Zion is a synonym for the people of Jerusalem, but seems to symbolize a particular section of the city filled with the poor and the outcasts who needed encouragement and hope (Mic 1:13; 4:8, 10, 13). Many scholars find verbal parallels between Luke's annunciation story and prophetic exhortation to the daughter of Zion, especially as found in Zephaniah 3:14–17. Mary would then sum up all the faithful of Israel and would receive in her Son all that was promised to these faithful as daughter of Zion. Those who disagree do not believe that the verbal links are clear. They also observe that texts which address the virgin daughter of Zion also frequently consider her with disparagement, as sinful and shamed, and not as an appropriate symbol to apply to virgin Mary.

Disagreement over the symbol of ark of the covenant would again hinge on the strength accorded to the verbal parallels. Many find in Luke's description of the Spirit "overshadowing" Mary direct reference to God's overshadowing the ark. They also find in Elizabeth's reactions to Mary and in the dialogue in the visitation story (1:39–56) a reference to David's bringing of the ark to Jerusalem in 2 Samuel 6. In that case Mary would be the new and perfect ark of the covenant, housing the perfect presence of God in her Son, and would be like every Christian who, with faith, brings God to neighbor. A number of scholars protest that there are not enough verbal connections between the two texts and that the dialogue in the story in 2 Samuel and in the visitation arise out of dissimilar contexts.

Whether or not Mary is directly portrayed as the daughter of Zion or the ark of the covenant is not of ultimate importance, for the same theme is developed in another image agreed upon by most biblical scholars, namely, that Mary epitomizes the poor of Yahweh in the Old Testament. This group, known by its Hebrew title of the *anawim,* was seen as the faithful remnant of Israel, that group of Israelites who remained faithful throughout the history of their covenant. The title originally described those who were physically poor, but it evolved under the influence of prophetic literature into a spiritual title, so that after the exile it designated those who learned dependence on God. To these anawim was promised the Messiah, and they were exhorted to faithfulness by prayer and sacrifice as they waited in hope.[2]

Luke casts his entire infancy narrative in the mold of the poor of Yahweh. The characters of these stories, such as Zachary and Elizabeth, Simeon and Anna, all represent the last of the Old Testament anawim awaiting the Messiah with hope. The stories are designed, however, to culminate in Mary as the perfection of the anawim. She contrasts with Zachary's doubt by her faithfulness as the handmaid of the Lord, open to whatever the Lord wants (1:38). She keeps all things in her heart, pondering them (2:19, 51), the image of the faithful anawim who receive and reflect on God's revelation. She brings the offering of the poor—turtledoves—as her sacrifice to the Lord in the temple, and she hears from Simeon that the sword of God's word in her Son will penetrate her heart especially (2:22–40).

In this presentation story she is also molded as a more perfect image of Hannah, presenting her Son as Hannah offered Samuel (1 Sam 1:24–28; 2:26). Finally, Mary is shown praying a canticle modeled on that of Hannah and of all the anawim of the Old Testament, declaring, "The Lord has regarded the low estate [i.e., the condition of being the poor of Yahweh] of his handmaiden" (1:46–55). In all these images Luke shows Mary as the crown of all the faith of the Old Testament. In doing so he presents her as the first of the Christians, the New Testament "poor in Spirit," who are to enjoy the Messiah promised to those who depend totally upon God in faith.

Prime Principle of Mariology

In these brief biblical sketches the foundations of current Marian theology were laid. We will return to some of the biblical texts as these pertain to particular doctrinal statements about Mary which we will

survey. Our first step now, however, is to show how the biblical data
in general leads to renewed theological teaching about Mary. We can
see this in the recent discussions about the prime principle of
Mariology.

Before considering this discussion, though, we should observe
that most of this theological development has taken place among
Roman Catholic authors. They take the biblical texts as description
of an historical Mary whose person we can know, even if only in attitudes, and whose person serves also as symbol of every Christian.
While Orthodox Christians would not disagree with these basic points,
they have not explicitly formulated them into a theology. Their attention to Mary has expressed itself in a rich Marian devotion, but has
remained basically unformulated in doctrine. Among other non-
Roman Catholics, with notable exceptions such as Thurian and
Anglo-Catholics, few agree with the Catholic view. Some Protestants,
with no concern for the actual person, would consider Mary as a pure
symbol for Christians. Even more would see the person of Mary as an
individual who perhaps came to faith after the resurrection but then
receded from importance as the early Church spread. We will have to
consider these differences in our chapter on the ecumenical aspects of
Mariology.

We concentrate now on those who consider the person of Mary
and Mariology an important topic of theological consideration, and we
look especially at new developments over the prime principle. The
prime principle is said to be that truth about Mary which connects all
the Marian truths and which also connects Marian theology to the
central mysteries of redemption. It is the foundational teaching from
which all the others can be deduced. It is the ultimate answer within
Mariology when one asks "why?" about any other Marian truth. This
first principle is also the connecting link with the rest of Christian revelation, for the "why?" asked of this principle finds its answer outside
Mariology and in the central truths of the faith.

Traditional Marian theology up to Vatican II stressed the Christotypical approach, a Mariology "from above."[3] In this view the prime
principle accepted by a wide majority of scholars was the divine motherhood of Mary. All other truths arose in function of this truth and it
answered the "why?" behind every title or role that we could attribute
to Mary. Even within traditional Mariology, however, this prime prin-

ciple had to be nuanced. There was already some sense of the biblical texts which stressed the importance of Mary's faith over her physical motherhood. This led authors to consider a prime principle which stressed Mary's active consent to her motherhood, a consent which had an effect on the history of salvation. Most understood this faith dimension as implied in the simple title of divine motherhood. Others spelled it out by a prime principle of Mary as associate of the Redeemer, or as mother of the whole Christ, or as spousal mother, to name a few.

In all of these instances, nevertheless, there was still a stress on a Mariology "from above," i.e., on showing Mary joined to Christ facing the Church in her role in redemption. More recent suggestions by scholars seem to redefine the prime principle. They want to keep from the Christotypical dimensions of this principle the concern to preserve a special role for Mary in redemption, but see the need to affirm this role by a principle with an ecclesiotypical dimension, showing Mary as part of the Church, receiving redemption herself. They claim that this emphasis actually harks back to an earlier portrayal of Mary, found in the Bible and among the Church Fathers before the divine motherhood came into prominence in the fourth century. Authors debate what this prime principle is, but all their suggestions define Mariology "from below."

Otto Semmelroth claims that the prime principle is Mary as archetype of the Church.[4] In this role she lives in her very person all that the Church lives, and is in this way symbol and model for the Church. This role begins with a faith which receives the Redeemer, but is also instrumental in bringing redemption to others, in the same way that the Church can be seen as receiving redemption, but also as the instrument of redemption for its members. Karl Rahner suggests that the prime principle of Mariology is Mary as the perfectly redeemed.[5] In this she mirrors Christianity and the ideal Christian, receiving the gift of God himself in grace-given freedom, with total commitment, and in such a way as to serve wholeheartedly the salvation of others.

Edward Schillebeeckx thinks that the traditional prime principle of the majority can still be kept, but he understands it in new ways which emphasize the faith of Mary from the Scriptures.[6] Schillebeeckx refers explicitly to the characterization of Mary, prototype of the Church, or Mary, perfectly redeemed, as prime principles. He claims that such titles are possible only because of the concrete fact of Mary's motherhood of the Redeemer, and so presuppose it. Nevertheless, the motherhood of Mary as it actually took place has a subjective side to it. It was a freely accepted and personally committed motherhood, which redeemed Mary as well as having effects for the redemption of all humanity. The prime principle, then, is Mary's divine motherhood, not as abstract reality, but in the concrete manner in which it unfolded. The role of motherhood and Mary's receiving redemption in faith are two sides of the same coin.

Most recently there have been suggestions that perhaps a search for the prime principle is the wrong approach altogether. Certainly, the disagreements during the entire history of Mariology would show that it may be impossible to formulate one single truth that could sum up all the others. Moreover, it seems curious that there is not a search for a prime principle in any other area of theology. This desire for a prime principle may be a relic of an era in which Mariology was too self-contained and isolated from the rest of theology.

In any case, Patrick Bearsley suggests that one concentrate on a paradigm for Mariology rather than a prime principle.[7] A paradigm is a "way of seeing." For example, the view of the atom as a miniature solar-system composed of many parts caused physics to abandon its approach based on the view of the atom as the irreducible underlying component of matter. Physicists *assumed* this view of the atom *before* their research, and it led them to a whole new way of examining the atom. The paradigm does not itself contain all the truths and is not itself the object of investigation. Rather, investigation is conducted in the light of the paradigm. Moreover, a paradigm functions until it encounters some phenomena which it cannot explain, at which point it is replaced by a new paradigm.

Bearsley contends that the paradigm of Mary as the perfect disciple is consistent with the central teaching of the biblical data and provides a perspective from which all the other attributes and roles of Mary make sense. It gives us a way of understanding Mary that acknowledges the traditions preserved by a Christotypical theology, but introduces an ecclesiotypical context for them. It thus seems a more suitable paradigm, unifying present insights, replacing the previous paradigm that adequately elucidated only a Christotypical Mariology. Bearsley confesses that the divine motherhood may be the prior cause of all Mary's titles, the first in the order of God's plan. However, in the order of knowing, we come to explain Mary coherently and consistently in the light shed by the biblical paradigm of the woman of faith or the perfect disciple. There may be new insights in future ages and, hence, the need for new paradigms. For our era this paradigm seems the most adequate for making sense of Mary in the mystery of salvation. We need now to look at what theologians are saying about the roles of Mary in the light of the biblical data and the paradigm it suggests.

3
Mary in Current Theology

While by far the vast majority of biblical studies concerning Mary stress the ecclesiotypical approach and a Mariology "from below," the doctrinal studies on Mary tend to retain some of the Christotypical elements of the tradition. The Second Vatican Council itself worked on a compromise by mixing the Christotypical and the ecclesiotypical approaches, though it moved toward and emphasized the latter. In the same way, current theology shows a mixture of approaches, but gives indication of a stronger and stronger adaptation of the ecclesiotypical approach. The emphasis varies in the different areas of Marian theology, but one has a sense that doctrinal studies are slowly and gradually absorbing the implications of new biblical insights. Moreover, proponents of this ecclesiotypical Mariology claim that their approach is a return to the earliest traditions of the Church. We will survey the theological developments by considering in turn each of the principal roles attributed to Mary in current Mariology.

Our sources for this survey include major periodicals, especially the journals published by the Mariological societies in Europe and the United States,[1] and the two prominent journals of Marian theology, *Ephemerides Mariologicae* and *Marianum*. There are, in addition, several prominent scholars who have written books covering all the major areas of Mariology. Since several of these authors published works just prior to Vatican II, their theology influenced the Council and provided the basis for present developments. We have already cited the works of Karl Rahner, Edward Schillebeeckx, and Otto Semmelroth in the previous chapter. We might now add the works of Hugo

Rahner[2] and René Laurentin.[3] More recent comprehensive considerations include works by Eamon Carroll,[4] Donal Flanagan,[5] and George Maloney,[6] and an encyclopedia of Mariology by Michael O'Carroll.[7]

The Divine Maternity

The area of Marian theology which is by far the most Christo-typical in approach is that which discusses the role of Mary as mother of God. Of its very nature the divine maternity sets Mary apart from the rest of humanity with a unique privilege, and associates her most intimately with Jesus. In many ways contemporary Mariology simply reaffirms the tradition, though in a more nuanced way. Traditional Mariology recognized that the Scriptures never say explicitly that Mary is the mother of God. However, the tradition claimed that Scripture said so equivalently: the Bible says Mary is the mother of Jesus; it also says Jesus is God; therefore, it says equivalently that Mary is mother of God. Contemporary biblical scholars nuance the truth of that statement, saying that the Scriptures indicate a trajectory toward full recognition of the divinity of Jesus. By this they mean that titles of God are attributed to Jesus in the Scriptures, but these texts do not explain *how* Jesus can be God. The final formulation of this truth comes after the New Testament era.[8]

Within the New Testament, there are a plurality of Christologies, only some of which indicate that Jesus is God. Moreover, when Jesus is called God in the New Testament, it is in a functional sense rather than an ontological sense, i.e., the texts are concerned with what Jesus does for us rather than with his intrinsic essence as such. Jesus is called God in recognition of the fact that he reveals a saving God to us in his being. (This statement is deliberately vague in order to reflect the fact that Scripture does not concern itself further with explaining *how* Jesus reveals divinity.)

This functional theology of the Bible points toward further definition which crystallized in the philosophical elaborations of the Council of Ephesus in 431 and the Council of Chalcedon in 451. During these years the biblical language was reinterpreted to express the very essence of Jesus as having the nature of God and the nature of man in one and the same person. When this final position was attained, then Mary could be said with fullest clarity to be the mother of God. The Council of Ephesus did in fact proclaim Mary *Theotokos* or "God-Bearer," and twenty years later Chalcedon clarified how, when it finalized the description of Jesus as one person with two natures.

There is an important conclusion to be drawn by Mariologists from this development. The divine maternity, the title *Theotokos,* is used not so much to say something about Mary as to say something about Jesus. To call Mary mother of God is not to say that she is in any way above or equal to God. It says rather that humanity and divinity are so united in the one divine person of Jesus that human characteristics and activities can be attributed to God himself. To deny that Mary is *Theotokos* is to say that she gave birth to only a human Jesus. This separates the humanity from the divinity of Jesus or denies the divinity of Jesus altogether. Thus, the doctrine of the divine maternity has been upheld to safeguard the truth that Jesus is God and man in perfect unity.

Recent Christology, emphasizing an approach "from below," finds the formula of Chalcedon in need of reformulation. The language has little meaning for contemporary society, and the formulation does not seem to allow enough room for a full treatment of the humanity of Jesus. In attempting reformulations, some current Christology has tried to stay close to the traditions, while some has become more radical. Each attempt has developed a different view of Mary's maternity. Where Christology has remained more traditional and has emphasized the unity of humanity and divinity in Jesus, then Mary's title is reaffirmed without difficulty. Where more radical Christology places a greater distinction between the human Jesus and the divinity which he reveals, there is greater concern with the title mother of God as an over-simplification. Mariologists will point out that perhaps *Theotokos* serves more and more the role it was intended to serve from the beginning. This title of Mary warns that the intent of Chalcedon needs to be affirmed even if new ways must be found to explain how Jesus is divine and human. New vocabulary must not end up expressing the reality in the inadequate ways rejected by Chalcedon itself.[9]

What we have said about the divine maternity thus far points away from Mary and toward Jesus directly. Contemporary Mariology, however, reaffirms another traditional aspect of the divine maternity which says something more directly about Mary. The focus of attention is the annunciation story and Mary's *fiat* ("let it be done to me"). This indicates that Mary freely consented to becoming the mother of Jesus and is thereby involved in some active way in the mystery of redemption. The Christotypical approach which still continues in current Mariology would describe Mary's *fiat* as associating her with Christ in working redemption. The *fiat* leads to other titles such as Mary's spiritual maternity. We will consider this role in a later section of this chapter. Nevertheless, theology "from below" has led to a new emphasis on Mary's *receiving* redemption. The divine maternity is considered from an ecclesiotypical perspective which shows her as part of the community of believers. We will briefly consider this perspective.

Eve-Church Typology

Charles Neumann has shown that much current study of the divine maternity has moved away from problems regarding the incarnation of Jesus and to concern with redemption and the Church.[10] Neumann confirms what Walter Burghardt said years earlier. He pointed out that the title *Theotokos* at Ephesus offered the possibility of honoring Mary as mother of God, but also as type or model of the Church. In honoring Mary as mother of God the stress would be on the physical Christ and his person. However, one can also stress the mystical Christ and his work, and so *Theotokos* would then center on Mary as type of the Church.[11] In this latter emphasis, which is the concern of today's Church, Mary's *fiat* is given prominence especially as her openness in faith to the redemption that her Son would work in her as well as in all humanity. St. Augustine summed this up in a phrase often quoted in Mariology: "prius mente quam ventre" (Mary conceived Jesus in her mind and heart before she conceived him in her womb).

Both Semmelroth and Burghardt give the elements that constitute a "type" in theology. The type must be a concrete representation or personification of another reality (the anti-type). There must be a real relationship that links the two and provides an objective foundation for representation. There must be a design (God's master plan) which is realized in both type and anti-type. Finally, the type is a moral example but also actually shares in the reality which it represents. By these elements the early Church saw Mary not simply as a metaphor for the Church but as intended by God as an objective representation of the Church. Mary lives in her own person the life joined to Christ that is lived by the Church. The real relationship is based above all on Mary's act of faith, her consent at the annunciation, which opened her to receive the Redeemer and his gifts.

One of the earliest ways of describing this relationship between Mary and the Church was the use by the Church Fathers of the concept of the new Eve.[12] The term is not found in the Bible, but is consistent with biblical thought. Taking its cue from the New Testament images of Christ as the new Adam, the idea of the new Eve can build also on the story in Genesis. The new Eve can be seen interchangeably as Mary or the Church paralleling or contrasting with the first Eve.

When constructing a parallel between Mary and Eve, the Fathers often incorporate the symbolic value of Mary's virginity as well as her motherhood, although at this point it must be admitted that the parallels are more strictly between Mary and elements of the Eve story, rather than between Mary and Eve as such. Mary, the new Eve, virginally gives origin to the new Adam as Adam virginally gave origin to Eve. On occasion the comparison changes: Mary is the virginal *soil* bringing forth the new Adam as the soil gave forth the first Adam. In either case, the stress seems to be on the new creation replacing the first creation, with Mary bringing forth this new life. Usually this loose paralleling with Eve is joined to a contrast between Mary and Eve. The Fathers stress Mary's obedience in contrast to Eve's disobedience, so that she counter-balances and frees what the disobedience of the first Eve placed in bondage. In this approach, the emphasis is on Mary's attitude as believer, her active faith response to the gift of life in her Son.

The use of the Mary-Eve typology enables one to combine Mary's role as mother and at the same time believer of the Word. It also leads to a Mary-Church typology, for the Church is seen as the virginal mother, bringing forth Christ in her members in the new creation (Gal 4:19; 2 Cor 11:2), while she is at the same time the faithful and obedient spouse of Christ who receives the gift of his love and his very life (Eph 5:21–33). Because of these comparisons, those who advocate an ecclesiotypical Mariology have a strong argument when they say that their approach is a return to the earliest traditions of the Church. Even the divine maternity can be understood as the highest expression of Mary as the woman of faith, the paradigm of the perfect Christian. The problem with typology is the difficulty of defining precisely the points of comparison. There is thus the risk of comparing too much. The Fathers were clear in avoiding one danger, that of making Mary equal to Christ as full partner in the work of redemption, as Eve was equal to Adam. Nevertheless, typological explanations remain cloudy, and are not exact theological explanations. The Mary-Eve-Church typology seems to lend itself to, and current Mariology seems to incline toward, ecclesiotypical definition. However, there are many yet who take a Christotypical approach toward the divine maternity, fearing perhaps that otherwise there will be a diminishment of Marian theology. The influence of the ecclesiotypical approach has yet to permeate these circles. Moreover, the divine maternity is seen as the basis for a further role for Mary in redemption. This leads us to consideration of the spiritual maternity. We need also to consider how the view of the spiritual maternity is seen differently from a Christotypical and from an ecclesiotypical perspective.

The Spiritual Maternity

Traditional Mariology has held that Mary's consent at the incarnation had ramifications in the mystery of redemption. Put in its most general way, the argument is: Mary brings forth the source of spiritual life for all Christians; the one who brings life is a mother; therefore, Mary is in some way our spiritual mother. Thus, the divine maternity leads to doctrine of the spiritual maternity. This latter role of Mary has been the focal point of Mariology especially from the beginning of this century, but even traditional Mariology has debated *how* Mary exercises her role as spiritual mother. The debate has drawn in discussion of Mary as associate of the Redeemer and as mediatrix of graces, as part of spiritual maternity, but even the Christotypical approach has shown disagreements over these functions of Mary. More recent Mariology has made fuller use of the Bible and has stressed ecclesiotypical perspectives as a way of explaining Mary's role.[13]

Until shortly before Vatican II, the spiritual maternity was thought to be a teaching not found directly in Scripture, but only implied. Now further consideration by many exegetes has led them to find this theme explicitly developed in the texts, especially in John's Gospel.[14] French scholars, such as André Feuillet, have been prominent in their Marian interpretation of John 19:25–27 ("Woman, behold your son. . . . Behold your mother"). We have already seen that many are agreed that this text shows symbolism beyond Jesus' simple filial piety and concern for his mother. The text shows Mary as a woman of faith, first in the community of faith born from the cross. A number of scholars think that the spiritual maternity can be seen even more forcefully through allusions to Mary as Israel or as new Eve. These scholars would thus find better scriptural arguments for the theme of the new Eve than even the Fathers of the Church.

John 16:17–22 is often used to clarify John 19. There Jesus compares his disciples' sorrow and subsequent joy because of his death and resurrection to a woman who has sorrow while in birth pangs, but rejoices when the child is born. Israel is described in the Old Testament as the woman whose childbirth brings forth a new people (Is 66:7–8). Eve is also told that she will bring forth children in sorrow (Gen 3:16). Perhaps all these allusions are in the mind of the evangelist when he calls Mary "woman" in John 19. If these are the intentions of John, then he indicates that Mary is the Israel who brings forth a new community of disciples in the risen life of Christ, or the new Eve who gives birth to Christ in his risen life and thus becomes the mother of Christian disciples.

These allusions seem stronger if the "woman" in John's Gospel can be related to the "woman" of Chapter 12 of Revelation. There the woman is clothed with twelve stars (Israel), gives birth to a messianic child, and then lives with her offspring of Christian disciples who bear testimony to Jesus. There also the woman wages war with the dragon identified as the serpent of Genesis 3:15, so that she appears as a new Eve whose offspring (Christ and the Christian disciples) complete the enmity toward the offspring of the serpent. In all of these references the "birth" described fits more appropriately the birth of Jesus into risen life and the consequent birth of the Christian community.

It must be admitted that exegetes disagree on the interrelationship of the texts we have discussed, as well as on these interpretations of John 19, especially beyond the view of Mary as woman of faith.

The allusions to Mary as Israel or new Eve are not perfectly clear. To make any application at all of Revelation 12 to Mary is problematic, because she is not mentioned by name. The "woman" seems certainly the Church with the *possibility* that the image of Mary is superimposed as a second image. Even the assertion of this point, however, leaves the further doubt that the "woman" of Revelation may not be related to the "woman" of John 19, and that the books may not have the same authorship. While the biblical data remains inconclusive on the spiritual maternity, it does yield one interesting insight: if there is any teaching from the Bible on this role of Mary it is always in the context of passages which apply equally well to the Church. The spiritual maternity of Mary seems best approached from the ecclesiotypical perspective, whether taught explicitly or implicitly by the Bible.

Pope Paul VI seemed concerned with this perspective when he declared Mary to be mother of the Church in 1964. Vatican II had diligently avoided this title, but the Pope promulgated it in the closing address of the third Council session. It was possibly a gesture of reassurance to those who wanted, but could not get, more doctrinal declarations on Mary, but it brought theological dangers. Protestants could see it as another excess of Roman Catholicism, leaving the Bible behind. Even within Catholicism many could interpret it as an excess of a polemical Christotypical Mariology that sought "new conquests," but ran the risk of implying that Mary was outside the Church as mother, rather than inside as member.

To avoid these dangers, the Pope introduced qualifications. He stressed that Mary is the greater part, the better part, the principal part, the chosen part, but nevertheless an integral part of the Church. He also balanced the reference to mother of the Church with references to Mary as sister by the bond of nature, i.e., as one who shares fully our human existence. In all this, the Pope showed that theology may speak of the spiritual maternity, but it seems best to do so from an ecclesiotypical perspective.[15] We should see Mary as mother, not as if she were outside the Church, as a Christotypical Mariology risked implying, but as identified with the Church, as an ecclesiotypical Mariology would stress. This contrast becomes clearer as further elements are introduced to explain how Mary exercises her spiritual maternity.

Associate of Redeemer and Mediatrix

The central question concerns how Mary is involved in the work of redemption. Traditional Mariology, at least from the fifteenth century, occasionally used the title "Co-Redemptrix" to describe this role. Vatican II avoided it altogether as unecumenical and as too open to misunderstanding. Associate of the Redeemer seems a better description, but even this title needs further explanation. Traditional Mariology began its explanation by distinguishing between objective redemption and subjective redemption. Objective redemption is the actual work of Christ himself in saving us from sin. Subjective redemption is the appropriation of this salvation by the individual Christian. Traditional Mariology, even in its Christotypical perspective, was divided on Mary's relationship to these two aspects of redemption.[16]

One traditional approach, continued by many still today, stressed Mary's unique role with Christ, different from that of any other human role. Mary was said to have a role along with Christ in objective redemption itself. Scholars of this viewpoint, e.g., Gabriel Roschini and Clement Dillenschneider, were always careful to stress Mary's subordination to Christ. They stressed that Jesus alone is absolutely necessary for redemption. However, God has freely chosen to make Mary necessary and has accepted her obedience in union with her Son's as meriting the redemption of the world. These scholars thus claimed that Mary's role is always secondary, relative, subordinate and only conditionally necessary, but it is a role in the objective redemption. In technical vocabulary, scholars distinguished Christ's role as meriting *de condigno* (i.e., in strict justice), and Mary's as meriting *de congruo* (i.e., by fittingness). To maintain this opinion and still preserve the truth that Mary is herself redeemed, Mariologists have had to posit two effects of redemption, the first in which Mary is redeemed by Christ, and the second in which the rest of creation is redeemed by Christ and the subordinate merit of the redeemed Mary.

Even within the traditional Mariology many scholars, e.g., Werner Goosens and Henry Lennerz, opposed this viewpoint. They said that the revelation of redemption did not show two effects and Mary's redemptive role would detract from Christ's. They did, nevertheless, see Mary's role as involved with the subjective redemption, with the granting of redemption to individuals. In an approach that was still

Christotypical, Mary was seen with Christ facing the Church and distributing the graces of the redemption. In this regard she was seen as mediatrix or dispensatrix of graces. It was a further question—and again a debated question—whether Mary's mediation was universal and direct or simply indirect. Some saw Mary as praying for each individual and then distributing each grace as intermediary between Christ and the individual. Others saw Mary as indirectly mediating grace insofar as her consent at the incarnation was also a consent to all the implications of the incarnation, including eventually the giving of grace by Christ to individuals. Mary would thus continue prayers for all, but her role in distribution of graces would be indirect.

These Christotypical debates continue today, and there are a number of scholars who advocate Mary's direct, universal mediation and her immediate role in the objective redemption itelf.[17] It appears, however, that an ecclesiotypical approach and the paradigm of Mary as perfect Christian, combined with advances in the theology of redemption, offer a somewhat fresh perspective.[18] Mary's role as associate of the Redeemer and mediatrix has been explained in the context of redemption conceived as merit. Grace is thus pictured also as a quantitative substance. Recent theology of redemption has suggested that Christ's act be seen not so much as offering satisfaction or "making up" for sin, but rather as making available for us a life of perfect obedience to the Father. Christ does not "balance the scales of justice," so much as insert us into his just life so that it becomes our own. In this view, grace is not seen as quantity of merit acquired by Christ for us, but rather the quality of Christ's own life given to us as our own life.

Now if such be the act of redemption, then it becomes difficult to see how Mary objectively merits grace as a quantity, or how she distributes each individual grace directly. If we are dealing with a quality of Christ's own life, then only Christ can objectively redeem and only Christ offers grace to us by incorporating us into his very life. Nevertheless, there is a way in which Mary may be said to mediate redemption, and this becomes clear from the theology of the Church with which she can be associated. Objective and subjective redemption need not be so sharply distinguished as in the view of redemption as a process of satisfaction for sin. If redemption consists in our being incorporated into the just life of Christ, then in a sense Christ does not actually redeem us until we are actually in his life. Certain aspects of objective redemption are concomitant with subjective redemption.

There are also communal dimensions to this mystery of redemption. Christ communicates his life to us by incorporating us into a community which shares his presence. Theology of redemption gives rise to theology of the Church which in a real sense mediates the presence of Christ. The Church in its entirety receives redemption (subjective redemption), but does so in such a way that it also becomes the means by which the life of Christ is offered to others (part of objective redemption). In that sense we are all mediators of redemption without ever denying that we also are ourselves redeemed.

Ecclesiotypical Mariology can build on this theology of redemption and the Church. If Mary is type of the Church or the perfect Christian, then she does in a more eminent way what each of us does. Her *fiat* was a faith response to the gift of redemption offered in her Son. It signaled her receptivity, the beginning of her subjective redemption. At the same time it was her first mediation of redemption for all creation. In this sense, her association with Christ in working redemption seems not limited to just the consent at the incarnation. Throughout her entire life she shared in the obedience of her Son and was joined with him in the culmination of that life in the resurrection. Her constant receptivity made her at the same time a constant associate in redemption. In that sense also, her involvement with the distribution of grace is not limited to indirect consent at the incarnation, but to a universal and on-going mediation. This distribution of grace, however, is not through a role *between* Christ and the Christian, but is through her unity with every Christian *in* the life of Christ himself.

This ecclesiotypical Mariology stresses the biblical point of Mary's *fiat* and not just her physical motherhood. It keeps her role as associate in redemption and mediatrix of all graces, but still respects Christ as the one Mediator through whom we are all saved. It shows Mary's on-going association with Christ, and shows her as spiritual mother, but still keeps her as member of the Church. Her mediation is of the greatest degree, but not of a different kind from the mediation of every Christian.

Immaculate Conception

If there is still disagreement over Mary's role in redemption, and still some difficulty in bringing the influence of ecclesiotypical Mariology into these traditions preserved by Christotypical approaches, the conflicts seem much more resolved in the current explanations of Mary's immaculate conception and assumption. While these teachings were developed much for the purpose of "new conquests" in a polemical atmosphere, they perhaps unknowingly preserved insights that can be valuable for understanding the mystery of redemption. This understanding comes from a marked shift toward explaining these events from an ecclesiotypical point of view. Whereas in the Christotypical tradition these events were seen as unique privileges of Mary to prepare her to be the mother of God or to reward her for this role, now these events are seen as signs of what will happen to the Church. They are indeed privileges enjoyed in an eminent way by Mary, but they are also privileges to be shared by every Christian in some manner.

The immaculate conception describes Mary's preservation from original sin from the first instant of her existence. Theologians have always taught that even Mary had to be redeemed, but her redemption was described as preservative rather than consequent. She was rescued from the bonds of original sin before their imposition, while the rest of humanity is rescued after it feels these bonds. There are some difficulties in explaining this mystery, arising from difficulties in new attempts to explain original sin.[19] Past explanations of original sin tended to suggest a quasi-biological inheritance in which every human being bore culpability for some sin at the origins of humanity. While this explanation accounted for a sinful world into which one is born, and while it accounted for the need of redemption, its explanation of the inheritance of sin was not very satisfying, nor did it distinguish well between personal sin and original sin.

Another theory in the past, attempting to avoid the shortcomings of this prior theory, saw original sin simply as the absence of grace when one is born into the world. While this distinguished original sin from personal sin, it did not account well for the power of evil grasping one born into the world, nor did it account for the social dimensions of this sin. Contemporary theology has thus evolved new theories which see original sin as truly a power of evil inside the person, although not yet personal sin, and at the same time a social condition of all humanity. It is explained as an impairment of human freedom affected by sin even before there is personal sin. These effects of sin are inherited as the sin of all humanity because human freedom grows in interrelationship with others and these interrelationships are sinfully affected.

These new approaches to original sin make it more difficult to understand the immaculate conception, since it is hard to see how Mary could escape being born into these sinful interrelationships that impair human freedom. Some Mariologists, like Edward O'Connor, say that the doctrine of the immaculate conception shows that these theories of original sin are inadequate.[20] It is also possible that the new theories require a reinterpretation of the immaculate conception. In point of fact, there has been little written directly about Mary by those who advocate these theories of original sin. It does seem that the heart of the doctrine of the immaculate conception is not in Mary's being different from the rest of humanity, but in her being prototype of all humanity redeemed from original sin.

Ultimately, the point of the doctrine is best seen from an ecclesiotypical perspective: however one comes to explain the eminent and unique aspects of Mary's redemption, it is a sign and a pledge of our own. Mary is from the first moment of her existence what we hope to become, at least by the final moment of our human pilgrimage.[21] Ultimately, the immaculate conception, like all the other aspects of Mary's life, says something about God and Jesus and the meaning of redemption. It shows God's fidelity and the love with which he surrounds humanity. Original sin shows an unfaithful world. The immaculate conception shows that even the accumulated sinfulness of the world cannot overcome God's desire to save. It reveals the beginning of a new creation and the worth of the human person. What God did in Mary offers promise to the Church and to each member. God called Mary and calls all to what is most human and most personal. He restores human freedom for a journey through life.

The immaculate conception was for Mary the beginning and not the end. It is the archetype of every Christian life and the reminder of what each can become, not from human power and initiative, but from divine. Since it is just the beginning, this privilege of Mary leads to a further teaching which has been part of traditional Mariology. Mary has been seen as freed not only from original sin, but from personal sin as well. Once again, this truth has been put into an ecclesiotypical perspective. The Church is to be holy; her essence and all that she comprises provides the means for holiness in her members. This does not mean that each of her members is fully a saint, but it does mean that she should be able to point to some who have already exhibited oneness with God in their lives. Mary becomes the crown of this witnessing. One is more redeemed by being preserved from sin than by being forgiven afterward. In this sense Mary is perfectly redeemed and is archetype of holy Church.

There are, of course, no biblical texts which teach these truths explicitly, but some exegetes believe the foundations are in those passages which describe God's mercy and his promises of redemption. For example, the authors of Genesis did not intend the story to speak of Jesus or Mary. The text cannot be used to prove any teaching about them. Nevertheless, the Christians who already possess their faith in Jesus may bring this faith to bear on the Old Testament. Their reading of the text is an authentic reading for Christians, since they believe that the final part of God's plan sheds light on all that preceded. With this qualification some Catholic scholars believe that the promise to the woman in Genesis 3:15 can be referred to Mary as the deepest fulfillment of the text. The authors certainly had no knowledge of Mary at all, to say nothing of events like the immaculate conception. However, they know of God's fidelity and his desire to save, and these can begin a trajectory that terminates in Mary as the sign and personification of the Church. The promise to the woman that she with her offspring will defeat evil reaches its greatest fulfillment in Mary's perfect redemption through her association with Christ.

In the same way the teaching on the immaculate conception is seen as building upon the pattern of continuity/discontinuity with the Old Testament. There is continuity with the Old Testament presentation of the poor of Yahweh who will be the faithful remnant of Israel. God loves them and his actions in history are designed as the gradual purification of this remnant. The redemption of Mary is the final step in this preparation of the remnant for the gift of the Messiah. Mary becomes the first of the new community, the New Testament poor of Yahweh who possess the Messiah in their midst. There is nevertheless some discontinuity in the new and definitive way in which Mary is redeemed in her immaculate conception, a discontinuity symbolic of the new and spotless Israel, the Church.[22]

The Assumption

Since the immaculate conception is the sign and pledge of what the Church is or will be, the Bible passages used to found the teaching are now most often passages speaking of God's mercy and redemption of humanity in general. A similar phenomenon is evident in current approaches to the mystery of Mary's assumption into heaven. It is seen as the sign and pledge of the final glorification of every Christian, and finds its elaboration in the biblical texts which speak of eschatology or the final stages of salvation. Mary is simply the first instance and most eminent example of the eschatological destiny of the Church.[23]

Besides the illumination that comes from seeing the assumption in the light of the Church, there is also further insight that comes from new interpretations regarding the meaning of eschatology itself. There is the insight, for instance, that eschatology is not just about the destiny of the individual, nor simply an escape to another world. It is rather a new creation which has social dimensions and which begins already in root form in the present. It offers a hope which creates possibilities in the present, possibilities that are political and social as well as personal. Mary's assumption is an affirmation of human destiny and possibilities, and is at the same time a challenge to act on that hope, to begin the transformation in the present.

The assumption "body and soul" is an affirmation of the goodness of material reality and asserts that the whole person will be saved. God does not just "save souls." In fact, many theologians and exegetes wonder if it is legitimate to divide a person into body and soul. They prefer keeping the individual as an integral personality: enfleshed spirit or spirit-informed matter. In that case, every person upon death receives a transformed body (not the corpse that is left behind), and is assumed entirely into eternal life, since soul cannot be separated from body. In that case, Mary's assumption is not a unique privilege. This point is disputed because of philosophical debate over how to define a human being. In any case, Mary's destiny is simply a public and eminent sign of the Church. Mary has been totally redeemed and shares fully now in the risen life of her Son. What happened to her is sign and pledge of the destiny of all humanity and of the entire new creation of the world itself.

One unresolved question of traditional Mariology was whether Mary died or was simply assumed into heaven. Pius XII's definition of the assumption deliberately avoided the question, using simply the clause, "when she had completed her life on earth." The question has still not been directly answered, but current theology about the nature of death sheds some light on the subject. Death is seen as a complex phenomenon with many sides. It is a natural part of life and can be seen as transformation of the person into a new existence beyond this history. Death can also be seen as consequence of sin, as separation from all that saves, and as filled with fear and mystery.

Mary's sinlessness and perfect redemption did not warrant exemption from death as transformation, though it did free her from the fear and obscurity brought to death by sin. Christ destroyed death as separation. Mary undoubtedly joined Christ in death as transformation. The assumption therefore reminds us that death need not be punishment. It need not be escape from material reality. It need not be the end but the beginning. Mary stands again as the perfect Christian reminding us that in Christ life and death are not undone by sin. What God has begun in the Church he will complete in final glory.

4
Mary in Ecumenical Perspective

Most of what has been developed in the preceding chapter as current Mariology has been the work of Roman Catholic theologians. It is not that there are no points that non-Roman Catholics could accept. Rather, there has been an extreme reluctance on the part of these Christians to develop any Mariology because of what they perceive to be the *centrality* of Marian doctrine and devotion within Roman Catholicism and an excess that slips into distortion. The declarations of the immaculate conception and the assumption as infallible truths seem to confirm a movement that will gradually displace Christ. These solemn decrees appear non-biblical and arbitrarily imposed by papal authority. Non-Roman Catholics fear that they will pave the way for further dogmas on Mary's co-redemption and mediation, whereby Christ will be displaced as unique mediator of salvation.

The previous chapter's presentation of Marian doctrine makes it clear that even Christotypical Mariologists have carefully qualified Mary's role in redemption and have subordinated it to that of Christ's. Nevertheless, until recently they generally ignored non-Roman Catholic misunderstanding of their teaching, using words like "Co-Redemptrix" which fostered that misunderstanding. Their often polemical theology also resulted in their developing a Mariology which was risky, although not erroneous, and which only recently is shifting toward a more fruitful ecclesiotypical emphasis. Moreover, while Roman Catholic theology may not have made Mary central to redemption, the same may not be said of a great deal of past Catholic piety. The practice, if not the theory, generated much misunderstanding and showed occasional distortion, until its renewal by Vatican II. Now there is the realization that ecumenism has to be worked at. It cannot simply be assumed that if truth is one, then truth about Mary will automatically lead to Christian unity. Indeed, the grasp of the truth is only partial and invites to on-going clarification, and the manner of expression of truth and its consequences for action are in need of constant renewal. Among non-Roman Catholics, Protestants are beginning to recognize that a total silence about Mary is itself an over-reaction of a polemical stance, and that even the original Protestant Reformers found place for Mary in redemption.[1] It cannot be said, certainly, that debate about Mary is now in the forefront of ecumenical discussion. There is still a great deal of clarification to be done over just how exalted a position Catholics give to Mary and over just how reluctant Protestants are in accepting any aspect of Mariology. At present there is even more need for the quieting of emotions. Nevertheless, the major shifts within Catholicism have invited tentative responses from Protestants so that both sides can begin the clarifications that can lead toward fuller ecumenical discussion.

Among those Catholic scholars who have authored books which deal specifically with the ecumenical aspects of Mariology, we can single out Thomas O'Meara,[2] Eamon Carroll,[3] and René Laurentin.[4] Some others who have written articles will be cited presently. Significant non-Roman Catholic ecumenists in the area of Marian studies include John de Satge,[5] J.A. Ross Mackenzie,[6] Stephen Benko (though his style appears somewhat polemical),[7] and the late Arthur Piepkorn who has left among his writings an excellent survey of Protestant literature on Mary.[8] Combined efforts of Catholics and non-Roman Catholics have borne fruit in the Ecumenical Society of the Blessed Virgin Mary.[9]

A genuine ecumenical movement is based on a return to the sources. We have seen in this regard that most of the emphasis in contemporary Mariology has been on the biblical foundations. This enterprise of exegesis has led to emphasizing an ecclesiotypical Mariology within Roman Catholicism. If the Lutheran-Catholic dialogues are any indication, there could be a growing agreement even among Protestants about Mary as woman of faith or the perfect Christian.

However, the difficulties loom large when one asks whether Mary the symbol is embodied in the actual historical person about whom we can continue to speak, even concerning her present existence.

This problem is accentuated as we move into Marian doctrine. While there are some few non-Roman Catholics who would be comfortable with this doctrinal development of Mariology, at least now, from an ecclesiotypical perspective, there are still vast numbers who believe further emphasis on Mary's personal role in redemption to be unwarranted. The disagreement stems from Roman Catholic movement beyond the explicit biblical text, which movement gives rise to the central questions of the entire ecumenical debate. In this regard Mariology becomes emblematic of the entire ecumenical movement, for it brings to the fore the same major issues that are decisive in all the other areas of theology. Clarification of these issues in terms of Mary may thus have ramifications in the long run for the unity of Christianity. In this chapter we will summarize these central areas of debate, noting however that brevity forces us to elide the considerable differences among non-Roman Catholics and to give simply a general sketch. We can, nevertheless, make a brief note here that Anglo-Catholics and, to a lesser degree, Lutherans find Marian theology more congenial than other denominations.

Theology of Grace

One of the primary concerns of the Reformation was to re-emphasize and maintain the absolute transcendence of God and his sovereignty in the work of redemption. This was expressed by the formulas, "God alone, grace alone, faith alone and Christ alone." The concern was a legitimate one in an age in which the emphasis was on human initiative, ecclesiastical practices, sacramental piety, and gaining of indulgences. There was need to return to an emphasis on God's initiative in redemption, and to an understanding of grace as totally his gift mediated by Christ and consisting of incorporation into Christ through receptive faith. One of the areas in which these issues crystallized was that of Mariology, and we saw briefly in the introduction how the issues became polarized. Moving beyond the polemics of the past, theologians are beginning to ask if a current Mariology can be developed which respects the legitimate concerns of the Reformation.

The concern of "God alone" through "Christ alone" is used by Protestants to criticize the doctrine of Mary's cooperation in redemption and her mediation. How can she mediate in any way at all without detracting from the unique mediation of Christ? We have seen that even Christotypical Mariology maintains Mary's subordination to Christ, but perhaps it still runs the risk of placing Mary between God (Christ) and humanity or of making her redemption different from ours. Ecclesiotypical Mariology seems fully to respect God's initiative and sovereignty by explaining Mary's cooperation and mediation in terms of the redeemed community. Her mediation is the perfection of, but is like the mediation, of every member of the body of Christ. Such mediation detracts from Christ's mediation no more than the priesthood of the faithful detracts from the one priesthood of Christ, or the goodness of the Christians detracts from God alone being good.

The concerns of "God alone" and "Christ alone," however, are also related to "grace alone" and "faith alone." God's sovereignty and initiative are also related to a particular Christian anthropology, i.e., to a view of human nature and of the manner of human involvement in redemption. Protestants tend to view human nature as totally corrupted by sin, and grace as the merciful disposition of God to forgive and to treat the sinner as justified. This theology concentrates so heavily on contrasting fallen human nature with grace that there is room only for God's initiative and for faith as confident reception of this unmerited gift. To speak of human cooperation is to underestimate either the radical nature of human sin or the absolute gratuity of grace. In this perspective the use made of Mary's *fiat* becomes a primary example of Catholic presumption of God's sovereignty, making God dependent on humanity or making a creature mutually effective with God in the work of redemption.

Roman Catholic practice has perhaps justified Protestant complaints because of its emphasis on merit and its devotional attitudes toward Mary, even if its theology was not officially saying the same thing. There is need of clarification, which could perhaps also effect some nuancing of the Protestant position. Catholicism tends to concentrate more on human nature as such and on the abstract or theoretical level, seeing it as part of the good creation that came from God. This contrasts with the Protestant concentration on the de facto historical aspect of human nature, seeing it as fallen nature. The Catholic

perspective tends also to see the faculties of human nature as historically impaired and weakened by sin, but not as totally vitiated. The
goodness of human nature can be restored.

Joined to this emphasis is also concentration on the *effects* of
God's sovereign action in the graced individual. From this perspective
there seems room to talk about the perfectibility of human nature. It
is fallen, but it can be perfected. Indeed, God effects that change.
Grace is totally from God's initiative, but it brings an intrinsic change
in the human person. Catholicism would thus give more importance
to the intrinsic effects of grace, while Protestants would be reluctant
to do so because they fear this would detract from God's initiative or
would not take sin seriously enough.

When the effects of grace in humanity are considered, then there
is also room for human freedom. Freedom is a grace-given freedom, a
radical change of fallen nature that comes from divine initiative alone,
but it is human freedom. Grace thus enables a response to God's
mercy and forgiveness. Faith entails not just a confident reception of
God's gifts, but a free engagement in the new life of Christ that the
gifts allow. Mary becomes the prime illustration of the workings of
grace. Her immaculate conception does not put her outside the absolute need of God's totally free gift. It does not prepare her to merit in
any way the role of divine maternity. Neither does her *fiat* express
self-sufficient contribution to the incarnation or redemption. Mary's
life simply reflects the fullest effects of grace which enable a faith-
filled freedom that responds to and engages in the sovereign work of
God in Christ.

Mariology thus forces a rethinking and a clarification of the theology of grace. Has Catholic theology and piety so stressed merit and
good works that it has created misunderstanding about the divine initiative and the sovereignty of God's grace? Has Christotypical Mariology been an example of this risky direction? Has Protestantism, on
the other hand, so stressed divine sovereignty that it has forgotten the
possibility of God's perfecting human freedom? Is that neglect behind
the rejection of Mariology? Perhaps clarification of these points will
lead to fuller dialogue over Marian theology.

It may also be that the ecclesiotypical approach will better
express both dimensions of the theology of grace. Especially from this
approach, the Marian question will be but the central example of the
theology of grace in every Christian. Mary will be the exemplary sign

that freedom does not substitute for grace, but neither does grace substitute for freedom. Mary could illustrate "God alone, grace alone," and the other Reformation themes, but in such a way as to show their primacy over the human, not their denial of the human.[10]

Scripture, Tradition and Magisterium

Another central area of debate that needs clarification is that of the authority of the Bible and its relationship to tradition and the teaching authority of the Church. Even after agreement could be reached that Mary's role in redemption is perfectly compatible with the theology of grace, the question would still arise: By what authority can such a theology of the person of Mary be established, since it is not contained in Scripture? Even the Orthodox Churches and those non-Roman Catholics such as Anglo-Catholics who accept some role for Mary within the Christian tradition balk at solemn definitions of the immaculate conception and the assumption as infallible doctrines of faith compelling belief.

As with other issues, so here there has been a polarization which only recently is beginning to be overcome. The Protestant theme of "Scripture alone" was a healthy remedy for the declining importance of the Bible at the time of the Reformation. However, this theme meant, as for the other Reformation themes, the primacy of the Bible and not its exclusivity. Statements by both Lutherans and Anglicans in their dialogues with Roman Catholicism show that many non-Roman Catholic theologians are recognizing that the word of God, the revelation of God, is transmitted by the words of Scripture, but transcends them. There is also the realization that the Scriptures are the embodiment of apostolic tradition and require that tradition to properly interpret the text. This offers new possibilities for the Marian questions, beginning with the recognition that even the Reformers accepted the traditions from Ephesus regarding Mary, and the doctrine of the perpetual virginity as well.

Inasmuch as this limited non-Roman Catholic endorsement of tradition provides some common ground with Roman Catholicism, it also invites all parties to enunciate better their understanding of the relationship of this tradition to Scripture. Vatican II has emphasized that Scripture and tradition are not to be considered two sources of revelation, as if one could find some truths in tradition totally separated from Scripture. Rather, revelation is understood to come from one source which is God himself. In fact, revelation *is* God himself as he communicates his presence to humanity. This presence of God is formulated in human words and concepts, but such human instruments can never capture the full reality. Revelation always allows for further enunciation of *the* Truth in human truths which remain partial and limited. The Lutheran-Catholic and Anglican-Catholic dialogues have shown that many non-Roman Catholics recognize in this stance of Vatican II a description of their own position.[11]

In this context, Scripture is the pre-eminent place where the Truth who is God is encountered in human truths. These truths are foundational for any further insights and are normative in that sense. Accordingly, Vatican II understood tradition as the living faith experience of the Church which preserves the truths enunciated in the Scriptures, but also explicates these truths, draws out what is hidden, and develops more fully insights consistent with but not wholly expressed in the biblical text. Perhaps as these notions of tradition are clarified in the ecumenical discussion, the Marian doctrines will be seen by all Christians as concrete examples of the dynamic interrelationship between Scripture and tradition. They could be seen as the results of the emergence of the Church's consciousness of faith as it reflects more deeply on the mystery of the word of God under the guidance of the Spirit.[12]

Related to this presentation of tradition is the role of the magisterium or teaching authority of the Church, especially as this is focused in the office of the Pope.[13] In the solemn declarations of the immaculate conception and the assumption, Mariology was joined to the question of papal infallibility as perhaps the greatest obstacle to be overcome in the ecumenical forum. Once again, however, clarifications are being sought and polarities are being drawn together. It is significant that in recent dialogues between Roman Catholics and both Lutherans and Anglicans, the non-Roman Catholic positions did not totally dismiss the papal office. Instead both sides said there was need to restate and to make more precise the role of papal authority, especially regarding papal infallibility.[14]

Current Roman Catholic theology has come to see that papal authority, like Mariology itself, must not be placed outside or above the Church, but must be seen as expressive of the Church. The affirmation of papal infallibility is part of the affirmation held in common by all Christians that God will not allow his Church to err definitively. By the same token, papal infallibility does not arbitrarily invent new doctrine. As Roman Catholic theologians currently discuss this papal function, they suggest that it gives official expression and formulation to what is already at least implicit in the faith of the Church. They also acknowledge that such papal teaching, while it preserves an important element of faith, may not always do so with the best explanations. Infallible papal teaching is not irreformable, and, in fact, requires the clarification of later insights. Many non-Roman Catholics seem open to these suggestions, but feel that further discussion is needed to make more precise just how the Pope discerns the prior sense of the faithful, and just how binding the papal teaching is on the faith of Christians.

What has already been made clearer is that even the doctrines of the immaculate conception and the assumption come out of a long tradition among the faithful, pre-dating even the Reformation, although that tradition is not unambiguous. Roman Catholics suggest that the tradition had to reach greater and greater clarity over history and that the papal declarations helped make explicit some teachings that have genuine continuity with biblical faith. They also observe that the Popes gave their teachings only after elaborate consultation with many Christians throughout the world. Non-Roman Catholics still question whether such teachings can be made binding on all Christians, but may not find these two doctrines totally objectionable, if the teachings are shown more clearly as consonant with biblical data. An ecclesiotypical explanation of these truths, as we have presented it, might begin the clarification sought by non-Roman Catholics.

As this central issue of papal authority is further discussed, especially in its relationship to Mariology, it might also be important to keep one other point in mind. One must distinguish those Marian teachings considered dogmas to be believed by all from those teachings still being discussed with freedom of opinion. Thus the immaculate conception and assumption are defined truths whereas the mediation of Mary is still being discussed. In questions that are not yet infallibly taught, there is freedom of conscience to form one's own opinion and even to dissent from official teaching when one has good

reason. In Marian theology much of what is being debated ecumenically revolves around teaching that is not yet definitive and therefore
offers room for forging a new common vision in time.

Hierarchy of Truths

The office of the Pope is essentially that of interpreter of tradition
as it builds on the Scriptures in the Church. All three elements of the
Church are intimately linked as vehicles for approaching *the* Truth of
revelation who is God himself. As such, all three vehicles share in the
limitations of human truth. Even infallible papal teachings are limited
by the state of human knowledge at the time of definition, by the
changeable conceptions and thought patterns of the time, by the specific motives in defining, and by the changes in meaning of human
language itself. We have seen how even defined teachings like the
immaculate conception, as well as other teachings from tradition, can
undergo shifts of interpretation, such as that from a Christotypical to
an ecclesiotypical perspective. Thus, even papal Marian decrees may
not be insuperable obstacles to Christian unity.

Vatican II developed a further concept to highlight the human
limitations of doctrine. This concept, described as the "hierarchy of
truths," has further ecumenical implications especially for Mariology.
In chapter 2, number 11, of the *Decree on Ecumenism,* the Council
states: "When comparing doctrines, they (Catholic theologians)
should remember that in Catholic doctrine there exists an order or
'hierarchy' of truths, since these vary in their relation to the foundation of the Christian faith." Undoubtedly, the hope of the Council was
that, even in the absence of complete accord, Christians could come
to fuller unity if they could achieve agreement on central teachings
while continuing to disagree on the peripheral ones. Unfortunately,
the Council did not explain the basis for determining the hierarchy,
and this is now a topic of discussion among theologians.

It seems clear that Vatican II was not saying that some teachings
were more true or less true than others. Moreover, there cannot be an
unessential area of Christian belief, since all faith is concerned with
Christ and his saving work. However, some truths are more immedi-
ately and explicitly connected with this foundation. The connection
may be based on the content of the truths. Some teachings are related

to the ends of Christian life, e.g., Christology or the theology of redemption, while other truths are related to the means toward those ends, e.g., theology of the sacraments and of the Church. Mariology would be seen as related to means, and perhaps as secondary or indirect means, and would thus be less central than truths concerning the ends of Christian life.

On the basis of this view of a hierarchy of truths, Avery Dulles has suggested that the anathemas or condemnations attached to the definitions of the immaculate conception and assumption be removed, since they accentuate division among Christians over doctrines that seem remote from the heart of Christian life.[15] Frederick Jelly agrees that the anathemas could be removed, since these do not make the teachings any more certain, but he disagrees about calling the doctrines remote. These peripheral truths throw light on the central truths by showing their application to daily existence.[16] They illustrate Christian anthropology, eschatology and the effectiveness of Christ's saving work. Thus, what is helpful in the notion of the hierarchy of truths is not the rendering of some truth as unimportant, but seeing all the truths in terms of their relation to the center. Bertrand de Margerie calls this development by concentration rather than by abridgement, i.e., concentration on the primary without elimination of the secondary elements.[17]

Sometimes the "hierarchy of truths" is related to the practice of the Church rather than the content of teaching. Some doctrines are considered more important than others in the affective consciousness of Christians and in their faith life. It can happen, in that case, that even defined truths may be peripheral to others that are not as definitively declared. It is also possible that there can be an imbalance of affection or devotional life that needs to be set right. The hierarchy of truths in the ecumenical discussion would then involve the setting in order of truths as they should be lived in practice, which could lead to fuller unity among Christians.[18]

Yves Congar has been the influence behind another interpretation of the "hierarchy of truths."[19] Consideration of the order of truths from the view of contents or from the practice of the Church can still lead to impasse. It is important to remember, however, that all truth of *something* is expressed by *somebody*. In the case of doctrine the *somebody* is the varied Churches and the historical forms that they have given to doctrine. There is thus a hierarchy that places the truth itself as more important than its forms of expression.

Edward Yarnold has given what seems the most radical interpretation of this suggestion for Mariology.[20] He says that doctrines like the immaculate conception and assumption have two levels of interpretation. There is the ultimate theological meaning conveying the central truths of redemption. There is also the symbolic meaning, which is the historical or quasi-historical formulation of the theological truth. It is possible that Christians disagree over the symbolic form of doctrine, while not disagreeing over the theological meaning. Thus, Roman Catholics could take literally that Mary was immaculately conceived and then assumed into heaven, but that is just the symbolic meaning. Protestants might not agree with that, but could accept the ultimate theological meaning that says God's grace requires response, provides conditions for response and results in sanctification even after death. There would thus be theological unity with a plurality regarding symbolic meaning.

De Margerie and others think that Yarnold's position nullifies the historicity of Christianity and contradicts the meaning of the doctrines as events. Nevertheless, Congar's suggestions seem a fruitful approach that has still to be developed thoroughly, but that may yet have important consequences for Mariology in the ecumenical forum.

5
Marian Devotion

Theologians have coined a maxim that contains multifaceted insights into the nature of Christian theology: *lex orandi, lex credendi* (the content of prayer is the content of belief). The maxim shows the importance of the liturgical and devotional life of the Church, not just as an added consideration for theology, but as having direct relationship to the doctrinal contents of theology. We consider Marian piety in this chapter because of this link that it has to Marian theology. The link of Marian piety *(lex orandi)* with Marian doctrine *(lex credendi)* is really that of a reciprocal influence. On the one hand, belief and doctrine express themselves in prayer and piety; on the other hand, prayer and piety give rise to belief and doctrine.

The maxim possesses strong ecumenical implications. For one thing, Marian prayer and piety is a strong element in Eastern Orthodox Christianity, even if its doctrine is not systematized and formally defined. If Catholic Marian devotion were renewed to express its doctrine more clearly, and if that devotion were brought into harmony with Orthodox practices, then Marian devotion could well provide the entrance into fuller unity with the Eastern Churches and could lead to clearer elaboration of an ecumenical Marian doctrine. The same may be said to a lesser degree of those Anglo-Catholics who accept at least a minimal Marian piety.

For the mainstream of Protestantism the *lex orandi* may be the first step toward the *lex credendi*, as far as Mariology is concerned. The liturgy is actually the primary place where the Scriptures are proclaimed as the living Word of God in the Church. The liturgy thus becomes one living expression of Christian tradition which contains and explains the Scriptures. As the expression of tradition, the liturgy can shape and develop doctrine from its biblical base. Protestants can, perhaps, come to recognize tradition more readily in terms of liturgy. Knowledge that liturgy included commemoration of Mary as far back as the fourth century of the Church might lead to more tolerance or even acceptance of existing Marian doctrine.

Donald Dawe has made the observation that our theological maxim has worked negatively in Protestantism. The original Reformers did not deny Marian doctrine, but were opposed to liturgical abuses in Marian devotion. Gradually, however, the opposition to abuse led to the elimination of all Marian devotion and liturgy. From the gradual erosion of Marian piety there came the gradual loss of Marian doctrine as well. If the trend should be reversed, so that the insights of Marian theology can be appreciated, perhaps the devotion will again be the way toward the doctrine.[1] Of course, much of what we have been suggesting hinges on the renewal of Marian devotion that is already underway within Roman Catholicism. Pope Paul VI issued a document called *Marialis Cultus* to serve as the guideline for this renewal.[2] The document offers a good commentary for what is being said and done about Marian devotion.

Primacy of Liturgy

Marian piety is to build on the biblical roots and the ecumenical sensitivities that we have described in the previous chapters. Accordingly, the devotion must be centered on Christ and on the mystery of the Church. Previous Marian devotions were not always remiss in pointing to Christ, but the accumulation of so many Marian prayers and practices ran the risk, or at least gave the impression, of centering on Mary rather than Christ. Moreover, previous Marian devotions, concerned so often with petitions to Mary or novenas, ran the risk or gave the impression of placing her between Christ and the Church rather than within the Church. Thus, Catholicism has reduced the number of prayers and services devoted specifically to Mary. Nevertheless, both Vatican II and Pope Paul warn against narrow-minded elimination of Marian devotion as the other extreme of exaggerated or superlative devotion.

The happy medium seems to be in focusing on the renewed liturgy from Vatican II as the mainstay and influence of all Marian piety.[3] In the past Marian devotion was seen by Roman Catholics as separate from liturgy, taking off after the official prayer of the Church ended. Sometimes it was brought into competition with the liturgy, when people, for instance, said the rosary during Mass with meditations unrelated to what was going on in the Eucharist, or when they conducted a novena to Mary after Mass. According to our new understanding, proper devotion begins in the liturgy, flows from it and leads back to it. This approach avoids implying that devotion to Mary is something that is automatically salvific. It avoids a sentimental or emotional devotion. It results in a piety that leads to action and to the gift of self to Christ within the Church.

Liturgy is not static ritual, but dynamic celebration. It is the celebration of redemption that renders that redemption present and that invites participation in redemption through faith. As such, liturgy centers on Christ, the source of redemption, within the context of the Church, the Christians who share redemption as a community. Technically, then, the cult of Mary is always related to the cult of Christ within the Church, just as Mariology is always related to Christology and ecclesiology. Mary stands as part of the Christian community, participating in the mysteries of redemption as these are made present in Christ in every celebration. She is ultimately involved in three major aspects of liturgy: commemoration, imitation, and invocation.

Liturgy is first of all the praise of God for what he has done and continues to do through Christ in the world. Praise takes the form of commemoration. One remembers what God has done, and, in the remembering, experiences God doing it again. Thus, each Eucharistic celebration recalls the principal events of redemption in the Eucharistic prayers that form the central part of each liturgy. In addition, the official prayer life of the Church is arranged in a liturgical year in which the various feasts highlight in order each event of redemption. Now in these commemorations place is given to Mary, as to all the other figures who are related to Christ in these mysteries. Mary appears especially in the Advent and Christmas cycle, but there are also special feasts in her honor. In all these celebrations the commemoration of Mary is another way of honoring God for what he has done in Mary and the other saints. The commemoration does not focus on

Mary as the end, but sees her as relative to God in Christ. Honor to Mary is adoration of Christ.

Commemoration is made in liturgy, not only to praise God for the past, but to thank him for what he continues to do in the present. It also allows us to enter these mysteries with our own faith response. Commemoration thus leads to imitation. Mary and the saints are introduced so that we might make their attitudes of faith our own, and thus join our response with theirs to the gifts offered through Christ. If Mary and the saints continue to live in Christ and if the Church embraces those in heaven as well as those on earth in one community, then the saints pray with us. If Mary is most eminent of the saints, then she is most worthy of imitation, and our own responses to God are united with her praise and thanksgiving. Thus, the liturgy of every Eucharist is dotted with recollection of Mary so that her attitudes may become our own, and so that our prayer may be joined to hers as to those of all the saints, yet still directed to Christ.

Communion of Saints

Although Protestantism has generally avoided mention of Mary and the saints because of abuses at the time of the Reformation, it seems open to the renewal of liturgy that allows for these figures within the context of commemoration and imitation. What still remains ecumenically problematic is the liturgical inclusion of prayer *to* the saints, invocation that would imply intercessory powers on their part. Protestants fear that Catholics attribute to Mary and others what is proper to God. They have thus tended to restrict the communion of saints to Christians on earth, understanding "saints" as Paul does when he refers, for instance, to the "saints in Corinth." This debate over the communion of saints is a reflection in liturgy of the doctrinal debates over mediation and over grace.

Exaggerations within Catholic petitions to the saints have probably justified the Protestant accusations, but there is perhaps more basis for theological agreement now that Catholicism has begun to clarify petition to the saints in a renewed liturgy.[4] Vatican II, in its *Constitution on the Church,* devoted chapter 7 to the eschatological nature of the Church and the union of the Church on earth with the Church in heaven. This paved the way for chapter 8 on Mary, showing that she is not only an eschatological sign, but also part of the communion of saints in heaven. We have not only an example of fidelity to be imitated, but a fellowship for our petitions. We should not render eschatology as totally unimportant for the present or as simply a future prospect in another world. There is no reason why death should separate the community of Christians. If the members of the Church on earth can pray for each other and share their personalities in mutual self-giving, the saints in heaven, and especially Mary, can be a part of this fellowship.

Once again, however, this function of the saints, like the role of every Christian in petition, is relative to Christ. It is only in Christ that there is any fellowship, and all prayer is offered in the uniquely efficacious prayer of Christ himself to the Father. Still, Christ demands response to his gifts. Grace enables our free offer of self to each other, including intercession, so that we may all freely respond to God's call to community in Christ. Protestantism is recognizing that even the Reformers acknowledged the communion of saints, while rejecting the abuses of the liturgy at that time. The 1979 International Marian Congress at Saragossa issued an ecumenical document signed by all the participants, Roman Catholic, Orthodox, Anglican, Reformed and Lutheran. They agreed that Christians can and should pray for each other, that saints do the same, and that Mary holds first place in this intercession, without affecting in any way the unique mediation of Christ.

Perhaps agreement over the communion of saints will be the way in which the person of Mary will be seen as having present influence in the Church, rather than being regarded simply as a figure from the past. While the ecumenical debate continues on this issue, Roman Catholics need to give precise context and clarity to prayers to Mary and to acceptance of her intercession. Frederick Jelly has recently suggested the guidelines that will help us keep the balance: Mary and the saints do not hear the prayers and grant the favors; Christ has the unique role of mediator. One does not approach Mary because Christ is remote. Since God himself is merciful, Mary and the saints do not function to make God more favorable toward us. The saints are not relay stations. Mary does not substitute for Christ. Mary is a subordinate means of grace, but not the source. We are not unworthy to approach God directly ourselves.[5]

Personal Devotion

Since the liturgy is not the only form of prayer in the Church, Marian prayer is not restricted to liturgy alone. Nevertheless, the liturgy sets the standard for Marian devotion as for all private devotion. If Marian piety builds on the biblical and ecumenical perspectives exemplified in the renewed liturgy, then it will be centered on Christ within the context of the Church. Bertrand de Margerie offers some suggestions about Marian prayer that may be adapted here as a summary of criteria for personal Marian devotion.[6] He modifies and reinterprets what seems to be a traditional formula for Marian piety, and speaks of prayer for Mary, with Mary, of Mary and to Mary.

The Eastern Church places a strong emphasis on prayer for Mary, a prayer that the Western mind finds difficult to understand. Why pray for one who is already in glory? It is a form of commemoration, praying "in regard to," and also expresses our desire that Mary and the saints receive continued glory from our acknowledging what God has done in them. Thus, Marian devotion should be *for* Mary, i.e., we should honor her, while always recognizing that honor for Mary is praise of Christ.

Prayer for Mary opens the way to prayer with and to her. For one thing, prayer for Mary also signifies an obscure consciousness that all pray for all, and that Mary is part of the body of Christ needing redemption as we all do. That prayer expresses in a temporal context a mystery which has timeless dimensions. It reminds us that our prayers are joined to Mary's and Mary's are joined to ours. This leads us to recognize that we pray with Mary, making her attitudes our own. Thus, Marian devotion in general is often a question of imitation. We live *with* Mary so that we might approach Christ within the communal context that he has created for redemption. Since Mary has such an eminent place in the communion of saints, our devotion is also *to* Mary so that the intercession *of* Mary might be part of our communal asking of God for the gifts of redemption and the final achievement of his work in us.

With the standard of the liturgy, then, we might summarize Marian devotion as being for Mary (commemoration), with Mary (imitation), and to Mary (intercession). This does not dictate which particular devotions are to be kept or eliminated, and decisions concerning that are dependent on individual choice, as well as the particular mentality of the devotee. What does seem important in renewed Marian devotion is that personal devotion remain personal, and not be the center of public practice. Thus, the liturgy has assumed the central position for public Marian devotion. Moreover, there should be respect for the hierarchy of truths on the level of Church practice. Marian devotion should be seen as secondary in that regard. Thus while almost every devotion could be practiced in a way that conforms to this standard, the multiplicity of devotions risks violating the hierarchy of truths on the practical level. The Church's recognition of this risk probably accounts for its discouragement of numerous private Marian devotions, and waning of these devotions is a healthy sign.

With the waning of devotion in prayer, there has arisen a Marian devotion emphasizing the imitation of Mary's attitudes. This has been especially biblically oriented, since the focus of imitation has been on Mary's faith, obedience and complete trust, reflected in her prayer and in her actions.[7] Mary has been seen as the perfect Christian who provides the model for contemplation and apostolate, for priesthood and religious life, for laity and families. In most of these writings we see the working out on the devotional level of the ecclesiotypical perspective of Mariology.

Apparitions

Before concluding this chapter, we should say a word about the apparitions of Mary. Whereas, in the past, devotion based on these apparitions seemed to hold a large place in Marian piety, return to biblical and ecumenical considerations has rightly reduced these devotions to a minor role. Apparitions can have a helpful role in calling people to essential Gospel themes, but they remain totally optional beliefs in the Church. They require thorough scrutiny to begin with, to verify their authenticity, but even after the Church has vouched for this, one does not have an infallible judgment of the Church and one does not have to accept an apparition as true.

In any case, even an authentic apparition can never be the source of new doctrines. What is of value in an apparition is not the secret or the unusual, but the Gospel teaching which it reaffirms. This can be contemplated with or without the apparition. Thus, the Church leaves its decisions on past apparitions, such as Lourdes and Fatima, as a minor and optional part of devotion. To make these apparitions minor is not, of course, to eliminate them. Visitors to Lourdes, for instance, are greatly influenced by the Gospel spirituality that prevails at the shrine, and such influence can continue to be beneficial. There has been at Lourdes, nevertheless, a shift of emphasis which renders account of the biblical and ecumenical concerns of today and which places Marian devotion into the perspectives that have been the focus of this book. Those who currently remain involved with preaching these devotions have tried to stress the Gospel themes of prayer, penance, conversion and healing, and to let the rest fade in importance.[8]

6
Future Directions

As with every healthy theology, contemporary Mariology continues to develop as it interacts with new discoveries and new needs in the Church and in society. Two areas of discovery and need are prominent today and are challenging Mariology to develop new insights that address these issues and that show the relevancy of Mary for humanity today. One such area is a new self-consciousness of the Church, leading to a greater appreciation of the role of the Holy Spirit. It challenges Mariology to show the relationship of Mary to the Spirit. This discovery of the Spirit has led to fuller awareness of the Spirit's work of peace and justice, even in this world, and of the Spirit's unifying power, making all one in the body of Christ. Such awareness has highlighted particular needs in the Church and in society, and challenges Mariology to address this second area of discovery and need, namely the liberation of the poor and oppressed, including oppressed women in a male-dominated society. We will now discuss these two new directions that seem promising for Mariology today.

Roman Catholic manuals of theology before Vatican II had no major sections devoted to the Holy Spirit, as they did for God as Creator and Christ as Redeemer. In some respects this was appropriate, for the Spirit is the dynamism behind, and is known in effects of, creation and redemption. The very nature of the Spirit is to be hidden. It is the Spirit *of Jesus,* forming him in the hearts of men and women, and teaching them all things concerning *Jesus.* Nevertheless, one can always gain greater appreciation of, and greater insight into, these rich mysteries by bringing them to conscious reflection. The lack of an explicit treatment in the theology books indicates a lack of explicit awareness of the role of the Spirit, with some consequent lack of insight. This lack came from under-emphasis of several aspects of Christ's presence and work of redemption. What was previously under-emphasized has now come to prominence since Vatican II, and has led to new consciousness of the Spirit.

A renewed sense of Christ's immediate presence and of the unfolding activity of redemption has led to increasing emphasis on the Spirit in the theology of the Church, of redemption, and of eschatology. The Church has come to be seen not so much as an institution in which Christ's presence is identified largely with the authority structures, but as the body of Christ. Thus, the Spirit is seen not just as inspiring the hierarchy, but as vivifying all the people of God. The theology of grace, formerly preoccupied with the created dimensions of this gift and its effects on human freedom, now concentrates on its uncreated dimensions as the very life of Christ. This has brought attention to the indwelling Spirit who makes Christ present. Eschatology, which dwelled on the future and other-worldly aspects of the Kingdom, is now concerned also with the anticipation of the Kingdom in this world. It thus dwells also on the Spirit who brings the Kingdom.

Contemporary theologians such as Laurentin frequently point out that Mariology developed during that time between Trent and Vatican II in which little explicit attention was being given to theology of the Spirit. Roman Catholics tended to assign to Mary roles that could also be assigned to the Spirit. Notable examples are found in the mottos or titles used frequently in Marian tradition: "To Jesus through Mary"; "Mary forms Christ in us"; Mary is the "Mother of Good Counsel, the Source of grace, the Consoler." These phrases can be assimilated to an ecclesiotypical approach to Mariology, though one must beware of misunderstanding or exaggeration. The point is that a more explicit theology of the Spirit leads to renewed interest in Mary, while a proper understanding of Mary requires an exploration of the relationship of Mary to the Spirit.

Mary and the Holy Spirit

Vatican II did not give formal treatment to the relationship of Mary to the Spirit, although it mentioned the Spirit about a dozen times in the chapter on Mary in *Lumen Gentium,* and once related

Mary to the Spirit in number 4 of the *Decree on the Missionary Activity of the Church*. Formal teaching on Mary and the Spirit since Vatican II has been influenced by new developments beginning in biblical studies. A large number of theological developments and applications in this area can be traced to the Catholic charismatic movement. A national Marian charismatic conference in 1979, at the University of Dayton, produced a book which brings together prominent theologians who have written on the relationship of Mary to the Spirit, e.g., René Laurentin, Eamon Carroll, George Montague, and Frederick Jelly.[1] Other authors who have treated this subject include Leon-Josef Suenens,[2] Heribert Muehlen,[3] and Christopher O'Donnell.[4]

In biblical studies the text that is central to considering Mary's relationship to the Spirit is Acts 1:14, where Mary prays with the disciples for the coming of the Spirit. Among the twenty thousand titles in the bibliographies drawn up by G. Besutti from 1947 to 1972, there was only one article on this verse of Scripture, and even that was of limited scope. Now the influence of the charismatic movement has encouraged new directions in study of this text and its context of Pentecost. In the verse itself Mary is made integral to the first community, waiting to receive the Spirit herself. Mary's relationship to the Spirit is fully in the ecclesiotypical perspective as far as this text is concerned. The link of this passage with other texts shows Mary as prototypical of the Church which is constituted by the gift of the Spirit.

Laurentin, for example, shows how Acts 1 and 2 parallel in many ways Luke 1 and 2.[5] Jesus' promise in Acts 1:8, "The Holy Spirit will come upon you," is anticipated in Luke 1:35, where Gabriel promises Mary that the Spirit will come upon her. The Mary in Acts, who is in the midst of a community filled with the presence of the Spirit (2:4), is the same Mary who in the infancy stories is joined by others such as the Baptist and Elizabeth, both "filled with the Spirit" (Lk 1:15 and 41). The community in Acts impelled "to the ends of the earth" (1:8) is anticipated by Mary who, in Luke's infancy narrative, is moved by the Spirit "to the hill-country of Judea" (Lk 1:39). Finally, Mary and the community who tell of the mighty works of God (Acts 2:11) are foreshadowed by Mary who prophetically "magnifies the Lord" after the annunciation (Lk 1:46ff).

Joseph Grassi has drawn numerous parallels between the Pentecost account in Acts and the Cana story in John 2.[6] Pentecost celebrates the feast of the new law of the Spirit, and Cana seems to pre-figure the gift of this Spirit. At Pentecost the old wine has run out, and the new wine of the Spirit fills the apostles to the point of over-flowing upon the crowd. Cana is a sign of this outpouring, as Jesus transforms the water of the Old Testament dispensation into the good wine of the Spirit and offers it in jars filled to the brim. Just as the Spirit at Pentecost comes to the apostles only after they listen to Christ and gather in his name, so Jesus at Cana offers the new wine only after the servants "do what he tells them." In both accounts, the mother of Jesus is there.

A final area considered by biblical scholars to be related to Acts 1 and 2 is the Calvary scene in John 19.[7] John uses this story to show the culmination of the work of the Spirit. When Jesus died, John writes, "he handed over his Spirit." At the same time, Jesus' side was pierced and there flowed out blood and water. All this happened only after the beloved disciple was included in the scene as symbol of the community of faith left by Jesus as his work of redemption. In John's profound symbolism we understand that the gift of the Spirit handed over by Jesus forms the Church, represented by the blood and water of the Eucharist and baptism, and personified in the beloved disciple. We note, once again, that in this scene, as at Pentecost, Mary is pres-ent as pre-eminent member of the Church when the Spirit is given.

This new consciousness of the role of the Spirit and its relation-ship to Mary in the Bible takes Mariology in a new direction. Mary is seen as the first realization of and the most eminent member of the Church formed by the Spirit. She is the finished work of the Spirit, manifesting the gifts of the Spirit and its abundant fruit. She prays in the Spirit, magnifying God with tongues, as did all on Pentecost, but praising God even more with interpretation that recounts his wonder-ful works. Her gift of the Spirit does not leave her passive, but moves her to action. She shows the ultimate sign of the Spirit by manifesting the love of God poured forth in her by the Spirit of love.

Ultimately, this theology of the Spirit avoids any sense of com-petition between Mary and the Spirit. They are complementary actors in the work of redemption, and both center on Christ as the focal point of their very being. Moreover, this theology shows that the comple-mentarity of the Spirit and Mary does not make them equal, but rather emphasizes the very human and totally subordinate role of

Mary. She does all that we have described her as doing in this book, but it is by the Spirit and through the Spirit that she can do it. Rather than seeing two juxtaposed roles in redemption, we see one. The Spirit enables Mary's role in redemption. It works from *within* Mary in such a way that all she brings of redemption comes from what she has first received. The Spirit forms Christ in her. As the relationship of Mary and the Spirit is more fully elaborated, it may be the way of confirming the ecclesiotypical approach to Mariology, removing any final traces of Marian triumphalism, centering on Christ as unique Mediator, and showing the possibilities of glory for a Church fully redeemed.

The word for Spirit in Hebrew is in the feminine gender and gives us a glimpse into the fact that God can be seen as female as well as male. The Spirit is also perceived as source of communion within the Church, so that there is neither male nor female, but a unity in Christ Jesus. Both these points about the Spirit have been highlighted in feminist theology which is developing in the Church. Mary also functions as a controversial symbol within this theology. Thus, the theology of Mary and the Spirit leads us to another new direction for Mariology, i.e., its development within a movement which raises consciousness of the subordination of women in both society and the Church, and which seeks to redress that situation.

Mary and Subordination of Women

Feminist theology is not concerned simply with theological content, but with the methodology of theology itself.[8] This theology does not seek just a compilation of discreet teachings on women as a subdivision of theological topics. It maintains, rather, that the entire way of doing theology is prejudiced by the presuppositions of a male-dominated society. Exposition of these presuppositions and advertence to the total human context (both male and female) which surrounds theological analysis will effect a new methodology, yielding new conclusions in every area of teaching.

The methods of feminist theology are traceable to two roots, one practical and the other theoretical. The first is the revolution in the life experience and expectations, especially of first world women. Society's progress in medicine, industrialization, and education and other advances have converged with changes in family structure and the ability to limit the number of children and to plan the time of their arrival. This has allowed women to move beyond the home and children to add or substitute other careers, and at the same time has exposed hostility from the men into whose careers the women have moved. Within the Church similar expectations of women have brought them to seek fuller participation in the decision-making processes, and have met similar opposition. Feminist theology has developed as that part of the feminist movement which seeks to explain within the context of Church and revelation this new position of women.

To help develop this new theology women have adapted a formidable analytic tool which is not unique to women, but which proves useful to their method. We have described this as the theoretical root of feminist theology. It is the philosophical insight that there is no such thing as value-free and totally objective knowledge. Theology, like any science, is influenced by the presuppositions that we bring from our own situations, including our social and political presuppositions. Thus, theology tends to reinforce the status quo of the life situation of those doing it, unless the presuppositions are challenged. Coming from a male-dominated situation, theology has within its content its own ideologies which tend to reinforce a patriarchal social structure. Feminist theology raises consciousness to expose the ideologies and to offer new perspectives promoting an egalitarian society, thus offering new theological insights at the same time.

Mary has been a powerful symbol in these ideological struggles, serving as an instrument for maintaining a male-dominated society, but offering at the same time a valuable image for feminists seeking to right an unjust situation. Authors who describe the ideological tendencies within Mariology and who also suggest alternative interpretations include Rosemary Ruether,[9] Elisabeth Schüssler Fiorenza,[10] Mary Daly,[11] Andrew Greeley,[12] and J. Edgar Bruns.[13] They consider many of the doctrines about Mary that we have studied in the previous chapters, but they examine them to uncover the presuppositions hidden behind them and to see if these doctrines cannot offer new insights consonant with a better understanding of women as equals of men within the Church and society.

Much of feminist Marian theology focuses on the title "Mother of God" and finds in it a Christianization of the myth of the mother goddess deeply imbedded in the human psyche. This claim requires that we first describe how some feminists understand the myth of the mother goddess to have operated in history. Jungian psychology seems to have given the first clues for this analysis, though many feminists see no need to remain in the Jungian system to reach these conclusions. To begin with, the mother goddess is seen as the religious symbol expressing the awe and ambiguity attached by archaic peoples to their encounter with the mysteries of life. So little was understood that almost all the forces of life were seen as sacred. Since the woman was so identified with the bringing of life, she came to be the natural symbol of all these forces. Archaic peoples would thus have had no difficulty in picturing a feminine side to God. Many feminists, such as Ruether, thus believe that what was expressed religiously must have been a reflection of the awe which man felt for woman. The mother goddess would thus have had a positive symbolic value, reflecting the equal or even elevated status of woman in the society.

The sacredness and mysteriousness of life, however, would also have had its terrifying aspects. What was not understood was also feared. The power of sexuality could be a disruptive force in society as well as a constructive one, and so the awe of life was ambiguous. Authors such as Bruns conjecture, therefore, that woman, who symbolized all these powers, was herself feared as well as esteemed. Because of this fear man, probably from the very beginning of civilization, sought to control these forces that could so easily overwhelm him. Sex came to be seen as evil, and woman, who was identified with the power of sex, came to be treated as inferior to the controlling and rational powers of the male. Religious instinct reflected this by attributing to the mother goddess destructive as well as life-giving powers. The good aspects of God came to be seen as masculine. The mother goddess thus came to be a negative symbol reinforcing the subordination of woman in society.

With this understanding of the meaning and history of the myth of the mother goddess, many feminists, e.g., Ruether and Schüssler Fiorenza, suggest that in the early Church Christians subtly took over the feminine images of God by assigning them to Mary the mother of God. Feminists point out that Ephesus, where Mary was proclaimed *Theotokos,* was also the city of Artemis, the mother goddess of the Ephesians. Mary came to replace Artemis in the popular piety of these

Christians. Thus, the development of Marian theology opened the possibility of returning to the positive symbolism of the mother goddess in an acceptable Christian form, and could have been the instrument for establishing an egalitarian society. Unfortunately, the religious symbolism of the mother goddess had acquired more complicated dimensions. While men no longer saw the goddess as evil, they did give her new traits that implied serious negative interpretations as far as woman was concerned.

According to feminists such as Daly and Ruether, even before the Christian revelation, male society subconsciously developed a more sophisticated domination over woman by reinterpreting the myth of the mother goddess. Rather than stressing her as simply evil, man came to revere her once again, but only by removing all that was a mystery and threat. Man developed the myth of the *virgin* mother goddess, so that woman could be separated from her sexuality and motherhood, which were still seen as inferior or even evil. Thus, woman was split into higher spiritual and lower biological forces. In effect, also, most women were then relegated to subordinate positions because their lives were predominantly centered on the lower functions of motherhood and the sexuality related to it.

The early Church followed this pattern in taking over the mythology of the mother goddess. Mary, who was seen on the popular level of the Ephesians as the feminine face of God, was seen as the *virgin* mother of God by the official Church. Celibacy was seen as the better way of life. The ideal woman, the nun, was contrasted to the large majority of women in the Church. In effect, anything that hinted of sexual differentiation was dismissed as of inferior importance, since the higher functions were ultimately those of reason and the mind. For all practical purposes the ideal woman was seen as masculine, developing what were considered masculine qualities, and, since the lower functions were seen as in service to the higher, woman was mostly pictured as in service to the man. Thus, the Virgin Mary came to function as a symbol to reinforce the subordinate role of woman in the Church as in society.

Mary and Liberation of Women

Feminist theologians have sought to make Christians conscious of what the feminists consider sexist presuppositions which influence the way in which doctrines are stressed. They maintain that one must begin to see sex as good, and that sexual differentiation is significant, but the significance is for complementarity and not for domination. Feminists also insist that woman should not be defined solely by her sexuality, when man is defined by his rationality. Rather, *all* should be defined as possessing *human* qualities. The woman has rationality as does the man, and the man embodies sexuality that has as much significant value as the woman's. Finally feminists also point out that sexual differentiation does not imply rigid mutual exclusion, but simply a different distribution of human qualities shared by every person. Every human being is a mixture of masculine and feminine traits. Recognition of this fact eliminates the sexist tendency to maintain that some traits exist only in women, which is also to see them as somehow passive and private when compared to the traits felt to exist only in men and seen as active and publicly approved.

Feminists believe that the symbol of Mary can be reappropriated if it is accompanied by raised individual consciousness and by structural changes in the Church and society. Mary can remind us that God is not just masculine as a power over creation, but also feminine as a ground of being and as the foundation of each unique person. Mary can also help the male to experience his feminine side, i.e., to learn receptivity. This receptivity is not to imply powerlessness or self-negation, nor is it simply a passive trait. It is rather the ability to listen to and to help others. By the same token, Mary's *fiat* shows that woman's receptivity includes an active element.

Some of the titles of Mary can be used to reinforce this point. Mary as virgin can signify that woman need not be identified totally with her sexuality, not because sex is evil, as was thought in the past, but because woman can have a self-directing autonomy which need not define her purely in relation to the male. Mary's immaculate conception, stressing her sinlessness, separates the woman from her association with sin and evil. Mary's assumption speaks about woman's body and about the earthy aspects of life or the material creation with which it is identified. In the past material creation, by its association with the woman's bodily existence, was associated also with sex, and all were seen as evil. The assumption says that woman, material creation, and bodily existence which includes sexuality are all the objects of God's grace and redemption.

Feminist theology is a fairly recent theology in the Church, developing as feminism develops in society at large. It is certain that not every feminist agrees with the line of presentation that has been taken above, nor can it be said that every aspect of the presentation has the same level of proven data to support it. Nevertheless, what has been said indicates the general direction of feminist theology and the possibilities of future direction for Mariology. What the end result of such a movement will be remains to be seen.

There are some indications that one result may be a rethinking of the role of women in ministry. Perhaps too much emphasis has been placed on Jesus as model for the male, and Mary as role model for the female. Such observations about this over-emphasis are not new, and have been made already in the past. Feminist theology reaffirms such views and urges that both Jesus and Mary be models for all of humanity, although Mary would obviously highlight dimensions of femininity in redeemed life. However, feminists take these general observations one step further and apply them to the issue of ministry. If Mary is model of all persons, then her role is not to distinguish women from male, hierarchical, priestly ministry, but to show the feminine dimensions of ministry in the Church as a shared responsibility of all, men and women.[14]

Mary and the Poor

The objective of feminist theology is not to transform society from a patriarchal to a matriarchal system. Rather, it seeks to move from male-dominated to an egalitarian society. In this way, it is also open to all groups within a society. Feminist theologians profess a close affinity with the poor and the economically oppressed, because women have shared similar social oppression. Likewise, there are further applications of the philosophical insights which have pointed out that theology is affected by the presuppositions one brings to the study. There are not only presuppositions of a male-oriented society, but also presuppositions determined by where one stands in the economic spectrum. People in a prosperous, middle-class, white society would tend to develop theological views that support the status quo of their position.

Liberation theologians have begun to expose the hidden ideologies that influence theology. Latin Americans, blacks, leaders of third world churches, and theologians who feel kinship with them have begun to point out that if one moves beyond blinding presuppositions, one finds that the Christian message makes a preferential option for the poor and oppressed. Preferential option suggests that Christian obligations of justice demand not just a general concern for all of humanity, but a special concern or preference for the oppressed. Liberation theology finds that Mary can be a symbol of this work of social justice, if one removes the prejudices that prevent one's seeing her that way. A prime example is given in consideration of the Magnificat, Mary's prayer in Luke 1:46–55.[15] If one moves past presuppositions which spiritualize the text, one finds that Mary's prayer is for the changing of social structures, for improvement of the plight of the poor, for social justice in this world.

Likewise, if one moves past ideologies which maintain the present economic order, one finds that Mary in the Gospels utters a *fiat* to a Kingdom that begins in this world and affects this world order as well as an after-life.[16] Finally, some liberation theologians are taking even the popular Marian piety of the past and transforming it into a powerful symbol of liberation. For example, devotion to Our Lady of Guadalupe is said to highlight Mary in the communion of saints as one still concerned with the poor and oppressed of her people.[17] Liberation theology becomes one final example, then, of how Marian theology remains part of the heritage of the Church, of how contemporary theologians are seeking to renew it, and of how Mariology points like all good theology to future and deeper insights into the mystery of God.

Notes

Introduction

1. For a detailed description by E. Carroll of the literature year by year, see "Survey of Recent Mariology" in the annual issues of *Marian Studies*. See also E.R. Carroll, "Theology on the Virgin Mary: 1966–1975," *Theological Studies* 37 (1976): 253–89.

2. J.B. Carol, ed., *Mariology*, 3 vols. (Milwaukee: Bruce Publishing Co., 1955–61).

3. For the history and brief analysis of the pertinent Council texts, see R. Laurentin, "The Virgin Mary in the Constitution on the Church," *Concilium* 8 (1965): 155–72.

Chapter 1

1. *The Mother of Jesus in the New Testament* (Garden City, N.Y.: Doubleday and Company, 1975).

2. *Mary, Daughter of Sion* (Collegeville, Minn.: The Liturgical Press, 1972).

3. *Mary, Mother of All Christians* (New York: Herder and Herder, 1964).

4. *The Birth of the Messiah* (Garden City, N.Y.: Doubleday and Company, 1977).

5. *The Gospel according to John*, 2 vols. (Garden City, N.Y.: Doubleday and Company, 1966–70).

6. R. Brown, K. Donfried, J. Fitzmyer and J. Reumann, eds., *Mary in the New Testament* (New York: Paulist Press, 1978).

7. Cf. G. O'Collins, *What Are They Saying About Jesus?* (New York: Paulist Press, 1983).

8. "The Meaning of Modern New Testament Studies for an Ecumenical Understanding of Mary," in *Biblical Reflections on Crises Facing the Church* (New York: Paulist Press, 1975), p. 105.

9. "Does the New Testament Give Much Historical Information about the Blessed Virgin or Mostly Symbolical Meanings?" *Marianum* 39 (1977): 323–47.

10. "The Historical Image of Mary in the New Testament," *Marian Studies* 28 (1977): 27–44.

11. R. Kugelman, "Mariology and Recent Biblical Literature," *Marian Studies* 18 (1967): 127–31.

12. See a summary article by J. Grispino, "When Did Mary Learn That Her Son Was Divine?" *Ephemerides Mariologicae* 15 (1965): 126–30.

13. H.A. Hanke, *The Validity of the Virgin Birth: The Theological Debate and the Evidence* (Grand Rapids: Eerdmans, 1963).

14. See *The Virginal Conception and Bodily Resurrection of Jesus* (New York: Paulist Press, 1973) and *The Birth of the Messiah,* Appendix IV.

15. *The Gospels without Myth* (Garden City, N.Y.: Doubleday and Company, 1971), pp. 80–82.

16. J. Craghan, *Mary the Virginal Wife and the Married Virgin. The Problematic of Mary's Vow of Virginity* (Rome: Gregorian University Press, 1967), and G. Graystone, *Virgin of All Virgins* (Rome: Pio X, 1968).

17. "Virginal Conception in the New Testament," *Theological Studies* 34 (1973): 541–75.

18. *The Virgin Birth. An Evaluation of the Scriptural Evidence* (Westminster, Md.: Christian Classics, Inc., 1975). See reviews in *Catholic Biblical Quarterly* 38 (1976): 576–77, and *Theological Studies* 38 (1977): 160–62.

19. R. Ruether, "The Collision of History and Doctrine: The Brothers of Jesus and the Virginity of Mary," *Continuum* 7 (1969): 93–105.

20. A. Clark, "The Virgin Birth: A Theological Reappraisal," *Theological Studies* 34 (1973): 576–93.

Chapter 2

1. "The Meaning of Modern New Testament Studies for an Ecumenical Understanding of Mary," in *Biblical Reflections on Crises Facing the Church* (New York: Paulist Press, 1975), pp. 91–95.

2. A. Gelin, *The Poor of Yahweh* (Collegeville, Minn.: The Liturgical Press, 1964).

3. C. Vollert, "The Fundamental Principle of Mariology," in J.B. Carol, ed., *Mariology*, Vol. 2 (Milwaukee: Bruce Publishing Co., 1957), pp. 30–87.

4. *Mary, Archetype of the Church* (New York: Sheed and Ward, 1964).

5. *Mary, Mother of the Lord* (New York: Herder and Herder, 1963), pp. 32–41.

6. *Mary, Mother of the Redemption* (New York: Sheed and Ward, 1964).

7. "Mary the Perfect Disciple: A Paradigm for Mariology," *Theological Studies* 41 (1980): 461–504.

Chapter 3

1. The United States annual is *Marian Studies*.

2. *Our Lady and the Church* (New York: Pantheon Books, 1961).

3. "The Blessed Virgin Mary," in A.M. Henry, ed., *The Historical and Mystical Christ* (Chicago: Fides Publishers, 1958), pp. 229–310.

4. "Mariology," in *An American Catechism*, an issue of *Chicago Studies* (Fall 1973): 295–303.

5. *The Theology of Mary*, no. 30, *Theology Today Series* (Hales Corner, Wis.: Clergy Book Service, 1978).

6. *Mary: The Womb of God* (Denville, N.J.: Dimension Books, 1976).

7. *Theotokos: A Theological Encyclopedia of the Blessed Virgin Mary* (Wilmington, Del.: Michael Glazier, Inc., 1982).

8. R.H. Fuller, "New Testament Roots to the Theotokos," *Marian Studies* 29 (1978): 46–64.

9. Cf. J.T. O'Connor, "Mary, Mother of God and Contemporary Challenges," *Marian Studies* 29 (1978): 26–45, and "Modern Christologies and Mary's Place Therein: Dogmatic Aspects," *Marian Studies* 32 (1981): 51–75.

10. "The Virginal Conception and the Divine Motherhood: A Modern Reappraisal," *Marian Studies* 33 (1982): 90–120.

11. "Theotokos: The Mother of God," in W.J. Burghardt and W.F. Lynch, eds., *The Idea of Catholicism* (New York: World Publishing Co., 1960), pp. 166–83.

12. G. Maloney, "Mary and the Church as Seen by the Early Fathers," *Diakonia* 9 (1974): 6–19.

13. T.A. Koehler, "Mary's Spiritual Maternity after the Second Vatican Council," *Marian Studies* 23 (1972): 39–68.

14. R. Collins, "Mary in the Fourth Gospel: A Decade of Johannine Studies," *Louvain Studies* 3 (1970): 99–142.

15. R. Laurentin, "The Virgin Mary in the Constitution on the Church," *Concilium* 8 (1965): 155–72.

16. A. Mueller, "Contemporary Mariology," in J. Feiner, *et al.,* eds., *Theology Today,* Vol. 1, *Renewal in Dogma* (Milwaukee: Bruce Publishing Co., 1965), pp. 109–128.

17. W.G. Most, "The Nature of Marian Mediation," *Ephemerides Mariologicae* 26 (1976): 177–94. See also the on-going debate between J. Carol (affirming Mary's role in objective redemption) and J.M. Alonso (opposing it) in the 1975 and 1976 issues of this same periodical, enough of which is written in English.

18. R.E. Hunt, "Our Lady's Coredemption as an Ecumenical Problem," *Marian Studies* 15 (1964): 48–86.

19. B.O. McDermott, "Original Sin: Recent Developments," *Theological Studies* 38 (1977): 478–512.

20. E. O'Connor, "Modern Theories of Original Sin and the Immaculate Conception," *Marian Studies* 20 (1969): 112–36.

21. R. Kress, "Immaculate Conception—God's Gift to the World," *Emmanuel* 85 (1979): 636–41, and "A Feast for the Broken-Hearted," *The Sign* 56 (1976-77): 7–10.

22. B. Schepers, "The Holy Remnant and the Immaculate Virgin," *The Bible Today* (1965): 1376–82.

23. D. Flanagan, "Eschatology and the Assumption," *Concilium* 41 (1969): 135–46, and H.M. McElwain, "Christian Eschatology and the Assumption," *Marian Studies* 18 (1967): 84–102.

Chapter 4

1. T. Harjunpaa, "A Lutheran View of Mariology," *America* 117 (October 21, 1967): 436–37, 440–41.

2. *Mary in Protestant and Catholic Theology* (New York: Sheed and Ward, 1966).

3. *Understanding the Mother of Jesus* (Wilmington, Del.: Michael Glazier Inc., 1979). The author also has many articles.

4. *Mary's Place in the Church* (London: Burns and Oates, 1965), chapter 5, and "Pluralism about Mary: Biblical and Contemporary," *The Way Supplement* 45 (1982): 78–92.

5. *Down to Earth: The New Protestant Vision of the Virgin Mary* (Wilmington, N.C.: Consortium Books, 1976).

6. See among his numerous articles "Mariology as an Ecumenical Problem," *Marian Studies* 26 (1975): 204–20, and "Honouring the Virgin Mary: A Reformed Perspective," *The Way Supplement* 45 (1982): 65–77.

7. *Protestants, Catholics and Mary* (Valley Forge: Judson, 1968).

8. "Mary's Place Within the People of God According to Non-Roman Catholics," *Marian Studies* 18 (1967): 46–83.

9. Its conferences have been published in various journals. A large selection of them are collected in A. Stacpoole, ed., *Mary's Place in Christian Dialogue* (Middlegreen, England: St. Paul Publications, 1982).

10. D. Flanagan, "Mary in the Ecumenical Discussion," *Irish Theological Quarterly* 40 (1973): 227–49.

11. P.C. Empie, T.A. Murphy and J.A. Burgess, eds., *Teaching Authority and Infallibility in the Church. Lutherans and Catholics in Dialogue VI* (Minneapolis: Augsburg Publishing House, 1978), pp. 23–26, and Anglican/Roman Catholic International Commission, *An Agreed Statement on Authority in the Church, Venice 1976* (Washington, D.C.: United States Catholic Conference, 1977), pp. 10–12.

12. E. Doyle, "The Blessed Virgin Mary and Dialogue with Evangelicals," *Clergy Review* 64 (1979): 347–57.

13. J.L. Heft, "Papal Infallibility and the Marian Dogmas: An Introduction," *Marian Studies* 33 (1982): 47–89.

14. P.C. Empie and T.A. Murphy, eds., *Papal Primacy and the Universal Church. Lutheran and Catholic Dialogues V* (Minneapolis: Augsburg Publishing House, 1974), and Anglican/Roman Catholic International Commission, *op. cit.,* pp. 13–16.

15. "A Proposal to Lift Anathemas," *Origins: N.C. Documentary Service* 4 (December 26, 1974): 417, 419–21.

16. F. Jelly, "Marian Dogmas within Vatican II's Hierarchy of Truths," *Marian Studies* 27 (1976): 17–40.

17. "Dogmatic Development by Abridgement or Concentration," *Marian Studies* 27 (1976): 64–92.

18. E. Carroll, "Papal Infallibility and the Marian Definitions: Some Considerations," *Carmelus* 26 (1979): 213–50.

19. "On the 'Hierarchia Veritatum,'" in D. Neiman and M. Schatkin, eds., *The Heritage of the Early Church: Essays in Honor of the Very Rev. G.V. Florovsky* (Rome: Pontifical Institute of Oriental Studies, 1973), pp. 409–20.

20. "Marian Dogmas and Reunion," *The Month* 231 (1971): 177–79.

Chapter 5

1. "From Dysfunction to Disbelief," in A. Stacpoole, ed., *Mary's Place in Christian Dialogue* (Middlegreen, England: St. Paul Publications, 1982), pp. 142–50.

2. In English translation: *Devotion to the Blessed Virgin Mary* (Washington, D.C.: United States Catholic Conference, 1974).

3. R. Laurentin, "Mary in the Liturgy and in Catholic Devotion," *The Furrow* 17 (1966): 343–65.

4. E. Carroll, "The Mother of Jesus in the Communion of Saints—Challenge to the Churches," *Proceedings of the Catholic Theological Society of America* 21 (1966): 249–65.

5. "Mary's Intercession: A Contemporary Reappraisal," *Marian Studies* 32 (1981): 76-95.

6. "Ecumenical Problems in Mariology," *Marian Studies* 26 (1975): 180–203.

7. See, for example, B. Albrecht, "Mary, Type and Model of the Church," *Review for Religious* 36 (1977): 517–24, and P.G. van Breemen, *Called by Name* (Denville, N.J.: Dimension Books, 1976), chapter 2.

8. R. Laurentin, "The Persistence of Popular Piety," *Concilium* 81 (1973): 144–56.

Chapter 6

1. V. Branick, ed., *Mary, the Spirit and the Church* (New York: Paulist Press, 1980).

2. "The Holy Spirit and Mary," in *A New Pentecost* (New York: Seabury, 1975), and "Mary and the Holy Spirit," *The Way Supplement* 45 (1982): 5–12.

3. "New Directions in Mariology," *Theology Digest* 24 (1976): 286-92.

4. *Life in the Spirit and Mary* (Wilmington, Del.: Michael Glazier, Inc., 1981).

5. "Mary: Model of the Charismatic as Seen in Acts 1-2, Luke 1-2, and John," in V. Branick, ed., *Mary, the Spirit and the Church* (New York: Paulist Press, 1980), pp. 36–39.

6. "The Wedding at Cana: A Pentecostal Meditation?" *Novum Testamentum* 14 (1972): 131–36.

7. E. Carroll, "The Holy Spirit and the Virgin Mary," in *Understanding the Mother of Jesus* (Wilmington, Del.: Michael Glazier, Inc., 1979), pp. 62–72, especially 68–69.

8. A. Carr, "Is a Christian Feminist Theology Possible?" *Theological Studies* 43 (1982): 279–97.

9. *Mary—The Feminine Face of the Church* (Philadelphia: Westminster Press, 1977).

10. "Feminist Theology as a Critical Theology of Liberation," *Theological Studies* 36 (1975): 605–26.

11. "Beyond Christolatry: A World without Models," in *Beyond God the Father: Toward a Philosophy of Women's Liberation* (Boston: Beacon Press, 1973), pp. 69–97, especially 81–97.

12. *The Mary Myth: On the Femininity of God* (New York: Seabury, 1977).

13. *God as Woman, Woman as God* (New York: Paulist Press, 1973).

14. J.M. Ford, "Our Lady and the Ministry of Women in the Church," *Marian Studies* 23 (1972): 79–112.

15. "Joy in the Revolution of God," in J. Moltmann, *The Gospel of Liberation* (Waco, Tex.: Word Books, 1973), pp. 113–22.

16. J. Alfaro, "The Mariology of the Fourth Gospel: Mary and the Struggles for Liberation," *Biblical Theology Bulletin* 10 (1980): 3–16.

17. V. Elizondo, "Our Lady of Guadalupe as a Cultural Symbol: 'The Power of the Powerless,'" *Concilium* 102 (1977): 25–33.

Suggestions for Further Reading

Besides indicating in the notes the central works of contemporary Mariology, I also tried to give for each section at least one reference which contained a synthesis of what is being said about that section. The following bibliography contains mostly additional works beyond the notes, for those who desire further reading.

General Overview of Contemporary Mariology

Gaffney, J.P. "A Portrait of Mary." *Cross and Crown* 27 (1975): 129–38.

National Conference of Catholic Bishops. *Behold Your Mother. A Pastoral Letter on the Blessed Virgin Mary.* Washington, D.C.: United States Catholic Conference, 1973.

O'Carroll, M. *Theotokos: A Theological Encyclopedia of the Blessed Virgin Mary.* Wilmington, Del.: Michael Glazier, Inc., 1982.

Vatican II and Changes in Mariology

Laurentin, R. *Mary's Place in the Church.* London: Burns and Oates, 1965.

McNamara, K., ed. *Vatican II: The Constitution on the Church.* Chicago: Franciscan Herald Press, 1968.

Napiorkowski, S. "The Present Position in Mariology." *Concilium* 29 (1967): 113-33.

Neumann, C.W. "The Decline of Interest in Mariology as a Theological Problem." *Marian Studies* 23 (1972): 12–38.

Biblical Perspectives

Branick, V.P. "Mary in the Christologies of the New Testament." *Marian Studies* 32 (1981): 26–50.

Collins, R. "Mary in the Fourth Gospel: A Decade of Johannine Studies." *Louvain Studies* 3 (1970): 99–142.

Isaacs, M.E. "Mary in the Lucan Infancy Narrative." *The Way Supplement* 25 (1975): 80–95.

Mary's Virginity

Jelly, F. "Mary's Virginity in the Symbols and Councils." *Marian Studies* 21 (1970): 69–93.

Piepkorn, A.C. "The Virgin Birth Controversy: A Lutheran's Reactions." *Marian Studies* 24 (1973): 25–65.

Vaughn, A.B. "Interpreting the Ordinary Magisterium on Mary's Virginity." *Marian Studies* 22 (1971): 75–90.

Mary's Motherhood

Grigorieff, D. "The Theotokos in the Orthodox Tradition and Russian Thought." *The Way Supplement* 45 (1982): 22–29.

Jelly, F. "The Concrete Meaning of Mary's Motherhood." *The Way Supplement* 45 (1982): 30–40.

Mackenzie, J.A.R. "The Patristic Witness to the Virgin Mary as the New Eve." *Marian Studies* 29 (1978) 67–78.

Richardson, H. "Mother of the Church: A Protestant Point of View." *Ephemerides Mariologicae* 27 (1977): 37–47.

Mary as Associate in Redemption

Chavannes, H. "The Mediation of Mary and the Doctrine of Participation." *Ephemerides Mariologicae* 24 (1974): 48–56.

O'Carroll, M. "Vatican II and Our Lady's Mediation." *Irish Theological Quarterly* 37 (1970): 24–55.

Mary as Fully Redeemed

Dawe, D.G. "The Assumption of the Blessed Virgin in Ecumenical Perspective." *The Way Supplement* 45 (1982): 41–54.

Macquarrie, J. "Immaculate Conception." *Communio* 7 (1980): 100–112.

Rahner, K. "The Immaculate Conception" and "The Interpretation of the Dogma of the Assumption." In *Theological Investigations,* Vol. 1, pp. 201–15. Baltimore: Helicon Press, 1961.

Ecumenical Perspectives

Cole, W.J. "Scripture and the Current Understanding of Mary among American Protestants." In *Acta congressus mariologici-mariani in republica Dominicana anno 1965 celebrati,* Vol. 6, pp. 95–161. Roma: Academia mariana internationalis, 1967.

Fuller, R.H. "The Role of Mary in Anglicanism." *Worship* 51 (1977): 214–24.

Kniazeff, A. "The Great Sign of the Heavenly Kingdom and Its Advent in Strength." *St. Vladimir's Theological Quarterly* 13 (1969): 53–75 (Orthodox Marian theology).

Marian Devotion

Carroll, E. "Mary in the Western Liturgy: *Marialis Cultus.*" *Communio* 7 (1980): 140–56.

New Directions

Brown, R. "Roles of Women in the Fourth Gospel." *Theological Studies* 36 (1975): 688–99.

Donnelly, D.H. "Mary, Model of Personal Spirituality." *New Catholic World* 219 (1976): 64–68.

Macquarrie, J. "God and the Feminine." *The Way Supplement* 25 (1975): 5–13.

Schmemann, A. "Our Lady and the Holy Spirit." *Marian Studies* 23 (1972): 69–78.

Other Books in this Series

What are they saying about Mysticism? *by Harvey D. Egan, S.J.*
What are they saying about Christ and World Religions?
    by Lucien Richard, O.M.I.
What are they saying about the Trinity? *by Joseph A. Bracken, S.J.*
What are they saying about non-Christian Faith?
    by Denise Lardner Carmody
What are they saying about Christian-Jewish Relations?
    by John T. Pawlikowski
What are they saying about the Resurrection? *by Gerald O'Collins*
What are they saying about Creation? *by Zachary Hayes, O.F.M.*
What are they saying about the Prophets? *by David P. Reid, SS.CC.*
What are they saying about Moral Norms? *by Richard M. Gula, S.S.*
What are they saying about Death and Christian Hope?
    by Monika Hellwig
What are they saying about Sexual Morality? *by James P. Hanigan*
What are they saying about Jesus? *by Gerald O'Collins*
What are they saying about Dogma? *by William E. Reiser, S.J.*
What are they saying about Luke and Acts?
    by Robert J. Karris, O.F.M.
What are they saying about Peace and War? *by Thomas A. Shannon*
What are they saying about Papal Primacy?
    by J. Michael Miller, C.S.B.
What are they saying about Matthew? *by Donald Senior, C.P.*
What are they saying about the End of the World?
    by Zachary Hayes, O.F.M.
What are they saying about the Grace of Christ?
    by Brian O. McDermott, S.J.
What are they saying about Wisdom Literature?
    by Dianne Bergant, C.S.A.
What are they saying about Biblical Archaeology?
    by Leslie J. Hoppe, O.F.M.
What are they saying about the social setting of the New Testament?
    by Carolyn Osiek, R.S.C.J.
What are they saying about Scripture and Ethics?
    by William C. Spohn, S.J.